Wilfred Owen's Poetry

A Study Guide

by

JAMES F. McILROY

Assistant Master
Barnard Castle School

HEINEMANN EDUCATIONAL BOOKS

LONDON

Heinemann Educational Books Ltd

LONDON   EDINBURGH   MELBOURNE   AUCKLAND   TORONTO
HONG KONG   SINGAPORE   KUALA LUMPUR
IBADAN   NAIROBI   JOHANNESBURG
LUSAKA   NEW DELHI

ISBN 0 435 18567 5

My thanks are due to all who have helped with this work, and in particular to Miss M. Gebbie, Mrs J. Martin and Mrs E. Mann, all of whom at some stage helped to turn a nearly illegible manuscript into a clear final typescript.

This little book is dedicated to my friend and former colleague, David Allott, whose kindness and universal charity will be an encouragement to all who come into contact with him as it was to me.

Published by
Heinemann Educational Books Ltd
48 Charles Street, London W1X 8AH
Printed in Great Britain by
Morrison & Gibb Ltd, London and Edinburgh

Contents

Preface

This book is designed principally for students of Owen's poetry at GCE 'A' level and in the elementary stages of university study. It concentrates mainly on analysis of the poems, though there is a section outlining his life and the influences upon him and his poetry.

Owen's total output of verse is small and most of what does not deal with his war experience is juvenile or unfinished. While it is not accurate to say that the war made Owen a poet, it certainly gave a sense of urgency and focus to his talents. For this reason this book is only a consideration of the war poems.

The most prominent aspect of Owen's work to emerge from this study is his diversity of view. His poems cover many aspects of a reaction to the war which is often too narrowly considered. The breadth of his attack on the war is usually underestimated, for his poetry is more subtle than the generality of readers credit. The pity and the sympathy which he felt for those involved in the war is demonstrated from a detached viewpoint and from as many angles as there are poems.

For people removed by two generations from the horror and impact of the First World War, it might be difficult to grasp its destructive effect on a whole section of the population of Europe. Reading Owen's poetry brings us closer to an understanding of and an identification with such a situation.

There has recently been a revival of interest in Owen. In an age which favours anti-war protest poetry, this is hardly surprising. Owen's poetry is protest poetry in the extreme, but it should be remembered that it is poetry first and propaganda second—that is what this book sets out to show.

For permission to quote from copyright material I am grateful to: Chatto and Windus Ltd for quotations from *The Collected Poems of Wilfred Owen*, edited by C. Day Lewis, and to the executors of Harold Owen's estate. Oxford University Press for quotations from *Wilfred Owen: Collected Letters*, edited by Harold Owen and John Bell. Robert Graves and A. P. Watt & Son, for permission to quote 'Recalling War' from *The Collected Poems of Robert Graves, 1959*. G. T. Sassoon, for permission to quote from the works of Siegfried Sassoon.

J. F. McI.

Introduction

Wilfred Owen, son of Tom and Susan Owen, was born on 18 March 1893 at Oswestry in Shropshire, and christened Wilfred Edward Salter Owen. He was the eldest of the family, with a sister born two years later, and brothers four and seven years younger than him. When Wilfred was nearly five the Owen family moved to Birkenhead, and it was there that he first went to school, at the Birkenhead Institute, in June 1901. The family finally moved to Shrewsbury in 1906, and there they stayed for the rest of Wilfred's life.

Owen was not particularly distinguished by success at school, and only after a time as pupil-teacher at a school in Shrewsbury did he attempt, and pass, the London University Matriculation Exam. As he did not come from a wealthy family, though, he was not able to go up to university as he really wished, but decided instead to spend some time as an unpaid lay-assistant and pupil of the Reverend Herbert Wigan at Dunsden in Oxfordshire. At eighteen, Owen was intending to take orders and enter the church, and it was not until January 1913 that he actually gave up this notion and left Dunsden.

From February till September 1913, Owen spent time at home and in Torquay, where he was convalescing after an attack of congestion of the lungs, an ailment that caused him trouble throughout his life. During this time he tried for a scholarship at University College, Reading, but failed to get one, and toyed with the idea of taking up another teaching post at Dunsden. In the end he went abroad to Bordeaux to teach English at the Berlitz school of languages from September 1913 till July 1914, and from then until September 1915 he served as private tutor to various French families. During this period war had been declared.

From October 1915 the events of his life can be even less detailed. In that month he joined the 'Artists' Rifles', and was commissioned into the Manchester Regiment in June 1916. In December 1916, he moved with his regiment to France; by January he was on the Somme, and within a few days he was in the front line of attack. After an encounter in April 1917, Owen was sent home suffering from shell-shock, and went to Craig-lockhart Hospital in Edinburgh to recover. It was here that, drawing upon the memory of the vivid experiences he had just undergone, he wrote most of his war poems, and, significantly, met Siegfried Sassoon, who impressed him tremendously.

By early September 1918, Owen was back in France where his regiment was engaged in fierce fighting as the enemy armies were withdrawing. On 31 October, his battalion was stationed on the banks of the Oise–Sambre Canal near Ors. In an attempt to take the canal on 4 November, Owen was killed.

Seven days later the Armistice was signed.

What this brief account of Wilfred Owen's life has not taken into account is his poetry: without that there would be nothing exceptional or particularly interesting in his life. Even as a child, he was determined to be a 'Poet'. As a boy of twelve, for instance, he was highly concerned in his letters with his grammar and style. Writing to his mother:

I also trust you will not show this letter to anybody, either, please. There is no grammar *nor* sense in this letter, I know![1]

All through his childhood, Owen would shut himself away for days to read literature of all sorts, poetry and prose. By the time he was fifteen, he had become so consumed with authors and poets and their work that nothing gave him greater pleasure than to search out people who had known or were distantly related to his author heroes. Writing to his mother in 1909, of a Miss Eckford with whom he was staying while on holiday in Birkenhead, he states ecstatically:

Miss Eckford's brother was a friend of Dickens . . !![2]

[1] *Wilfred Owen Collected Letters* Ed. Harold Owen and John Bell, Oxford University Press, London 1967, p. 24.
[2] *Letters*, p. 50.

In the same tone he writes to his mother that he has discovered, while on holiday in Torquay in 1910, a Miss Christabel Coleridge:

> *a descendant of Coleridge.* . . . I promptly discovered the house by means of a directory, and a few minutes later my heart (liver and cerebellum included) was hovering round her dwelling place![1]

Though Owen had no formal academic training, and no directed course of reading, he avidly consumed almost any books he could obtain. At eighteen he was writing letters which were stuffed with literary allusions and quotations. His letters by this time, however, had taken a deeper turn: he began to discuss literature more and, largely influenced by what he was currently reading, he became more sceptical, questioning his previously held opinions and his religious beliefs. In one letter of 1911, he quotes from Shakespeare, Wordsworth, Shelley and Keats.[2] The three latter, Romantic poets had an enormous effect on Owen and on his poetry, though not always a beneficial effect, where Keats is concerned. Before looking at Owen's devotion to Keats, it is important to consider the living person who most mattered to him, and indirectly to his poetry: his mother.

It was to his mother that Owen addressed 554 of his 673 known letters, and to whom he first revealed most of his poems. Susan Owen responded to her son's efforts by returning encouragement and faith in his ability. From Wilfred's letters, and from Harold Owen's autobiography, *Journey from Obscurity*,[3] Susan Owen emerges as the quiet driving-force behind the Owen family; a woman of much intelligence, charm and personal authority. Wilfred's dependence on his mother never slackened: right to the end, all the details of the war which the security arrangements permitted him to disclose were meticulously sent to her in frequent letters. In peace-time he wrote nearly every day when he was away from home, and in war he wrote as often as he could. The letters touched on all subjects, from her visits to the dentist to her views on his latest poems. The one consistent factor

[1] *Letters*, p. 61.
[2] *Letters*, p. 73.
[3] *Journey from Obscurity: Wilfred Owen 1893–1918*, 3 Vols., Oxford University Press, London 1965.

in all the letters is the great affection that Owen felt towards his
mother and which she reciprocated in like manner. She preserved
all his manuscripts and letters intact and made every effort to
publish and advance her son's work. Her letters to Owen are not
printed, but it may be safe to guess, judging from the responses
which they provoked, that they were equally confidential and
affectionate.

Altogether, the picture which emerges from the correspondence
between son and mother is of an obsessively close relationship—
over-protective on the one hand and over-reliant on the other.
In June 1913, he wrote to her:

> Objectionable men, and delusive, drive me back upon myself
> and Keats; unlovable women, and girls incapable of sympathy,
> drive me back to you.[1]

Again to her he wrote:

> All women, without exception, *annoy* me.[1]

These letters were written by a young man of twenty, already
displaying a studied and self-conscious attitude towards whatever
he wrote (e.g. the use of the rather affected 'delusive') and an
emotional dependence on his mother that is somewhat out of
place. It is true to say, I believe, that Owen, certainly up till his
war experiences, was in fact a sort of emotional Peter Pan. He
did not grow to adult maturity although the fact of the war and
its horrors shocked him into an awareness of real life.

One factor which does emerge from the quotation above is the
importance of Keats for Owen. Of all the Romantic poets, Keats
is perhaps the one who for most modern readers writes the
highest, most sensuous, most recognizably 'poetic' verse. It is
hardly surprising, then, that as a young man with a taste for
reading poetry, it was Keats who captured Owen's imagination.
The reverberations of its impact can be felt all through Owen's
poetry. By the time that the war broke out, there is no doubt that
Owen had read a great deal of Keats' output, but he had read
it in a highly non-critical way. Owen's devotion to Keats was
worship—and this excluded any awareness of the latter's weaknesses. His war poems often suffer because they are written with

[1] *Letters*, p. 191.   [2] *Letters*, p. 234.

the sound of the lines dominating the sense, and examples of this will emerge in the analysis section.

Owen's letters abound with references to Keats. A few examples might illustrate how deep his adulation went, and simultaneously show just what Owen found were his poetic criteria. It should be remembered that Owen was in no way especially trained or educated in literary appreciation, and though he was a sensitive young man with a determination to write poetry, he was often a poor critic of his own and other people's work.

> I still hold the violin capable of 'better' i.e. more essential, music than the organ, and *shall* do. While I hold Keats a more poetical poet than Milton.[1]

One can only assume that by 'poetical', Owen meant a poet who writes in a more self-conscious, romantic, sensuous vein. In this sense alone Milton could be put second to Keats, but it would be absurd to consider the two together thus. Owen fails to take into account the totally different periods in which the two wrote; he ignores the differences in their subject-matter, and fails to mention the differences in the intentions behind their work. The analogy to the violin and organ may well hold true, because as one will produce flowing melody but within a limited range of sound and effect, the other has a majesty, scope, range, and power to which the former could not aspire. This is not to say, though, that either instrument is better than the other. Owen himself is conscious of this distinction between these two poets when he says that 'better' stands for 'more essential', which in turn we can only interpret as more personally appealing.

Owen's judgement, in other words, is totally subjective.

Perhaps Owen's idea of how a poet should work is best clarified by yet another reference to Keats from his letters:

> Truly, if I found myself in a fair way to becoming a London surgeon, I should not, as Keats did, throw it up, and trust to the voices and visions. . . .[2]

Owen's idea that poetry is dependent on 'voices and visions' is a most revealing one. He may well have imagined Keats' poetry

---

[1] *Letters*, p. 350.   [2] *Letters*, p. 316.

springing from voices within him, but more than a vision was required to put together 'Endymion' or the various Odes. The aspect of Keats' work that Owen most obviously underestimates is his craftmanship.

The final point about Owen and Keats that I would make is that Owen saw himself following in a common literary tradition to Keats—as a perpetuator of Keats' literary principles.

Do you know what would hold me together in a battlefield? The sense that I was perpetuating the language in which Keats and the rest of them wrote![1]

It is significant that Owen should have looked upon himself as filling this role. In this last quotation, it is the *language* that Owen comments upon, since that was what most struck him in Keats' poetry. He seems not to understand that Keats does not discard the sense of his lines for the sound of the words. Consequently we have many places where Owen distorts (or loses) his meaning, for an alliterative line or a mellifluous figure of speech.

These two great influences on Owen, his mother and Keats, cover two sides of his personality which came together when he wrote, appropriately to his mother:

But never fear: thank Home, and Poetry, and the FORCE behind both. And rejoice with me that a calmer time has come for me; and that fifty blandishments cannot move me like ten notes of a violin or a line of Keats.[2]

A further influence ought also to be mentioned, before passing on to the war itself and its effect on Owen: the personality and poetry of Siegfried Sassoon.

Owen first met Sassoon when he was sent to convalesce at Craiglockhart Hospital. Having read some of Sassoon's poetry, he was intensely anxious to make his acquaintance. He did not have the courage, however, to approach Sassoon straight away, and it took two attempts before he actually broached the subject of poetry. In August 1917, he wrote to his cousin:

At last I have an event worth a letter. I have beknown myself to Siegfried Sassoon. Went to him last night (my second call) . . . He is very tall and stately.[3]

[1] *Letters*, p. 300.   [2] *Letters*, p. 234.   [3] *Letters*, p. 485.

Sassoon looked over Owen's poems, and though he disliked many early verses, approved strongly of many later ones. As they became more friendly, Owen became more dependent upon Sassoon's approval:

> But a word from Sassoon, though he is not a cheery dog himself, makes me cut capers of pleasure.[1]

The relationship which grew between these two was certainly one based on hero-worship on Owen's part:

> The *Man* is tall and noble looking . . . The *Friend* is intensely sympathetic . . . As for the *Poet* you know my judgement.[2]

His judgement of Sassoon as a poet was stuffed with superlatives of praise:

> I have just been reading Siegfried Sassoon, and am feeling at a very high pitch of emotion. Nothing like his trench life sketches has even been written or will be written. Shakespeare reads vapid after these. Not of course because Sassoon is a greater artist, but because of the subject, I mean.[3]

Sassoon's influence was soon to show its impact. In the same letter of August 1917, quoted above, Owen included a poem, 'The Dead-Beat' which he stated to be 'something in Sassoon's style', and it is indeed noticeably in the colloquial and satirical style so much used by Sassoon.

Sassoon's greatest influence, however, was to give Owen self-confidence. Sassoon was a fellow-poet who would criticize Owen's work and give encouragement and recognition to the younger poet. To be recognized as a fellow-poet by Sassoon was help enough for Owen. In November 1917, he wrote to Sassoon:

> Know that since mid-September when you still regarded me as a tiresome little knocker on your door, I held you as Keats + Christ + Elijah + my Colonel + my father confessor + Amenophis IV in profile. What's that mathematically?[4]

Without attempting to answer Owen's question, we can at least form a sum of his opinions on Sassoon. *Keats*, for Owen, signified

[1] *Letters*, p. 489.   [2] *Letters*, p. 494.
[3] *Letters*, p. 484.   [4] *Letters*, p. 505,

the ideal genius and poet; *Christ* is a saviour, dying for his support
of truth against the Pharisees; *Elijah*, a prophet; his *Colonel*, a
man for whom Owen holds a sort of *Boys' Own World*, hero-
worship respect; *father confessor* shows Owen's dependence for
backing and support; *Amenophis IV* (an Egyptian Pharoah)
possessed a remarkable type of classical physical beauty and
suggests Owen's attraction to Sassoon's appearance. Whatever
the answer to this sum is mathematically, emotionally it indicates
a high level of attachment and dependence. Owen summed it up
himself in the same letter:

> In effect it is this: that I love you dispassionately, so much, so
> *very* much, dear Fellow . . .[1]

While it is not difficult to see the personal effect which Sassoon
had on Owen, it is not so easy to find a lasting influence on
Owen's work. Owen had developed a Keatsian, lyrical attitude
towards poetry and apart from the inclusion of some lines of
direct speech and a few colloquial expressions which are usually
somewhat ill-fitting, he adhered to his elegiac style in spite of his
admiration for Sassoon's work. He did occasionally adopt a
satirical vein, but again this did not suit his range of feelings and
he returned to his more serious style. Governed always by the
highly emotional nature of his subject-matter, Owen seemed to
find an ironic approach too flippant. It lacked the sonority he
needed to attune with his subject.

What made Owen the poet we know today was the First World
War. His poems up until his war experiences often display a
promising few lines, but generally they are derivative, highly
Georgian verses. Accepting his complete works as the seventy-nine
whole poems and fragments which appear in C. Day Lewis's
edition of Owen's *Collected Poems*,[2] it is obvious that only the war
poems are of lasting merit.

Owen was twenty-one when the war began, and was living in
France. From the early days of the war, even before he had
enlisted, he knew what horrors war could create. Writing to his
brother Harold in September 1914, he said:

---

[1] *Letters*, p. 505.
[2] *The Collected Poems of Wilfred Owen* Ed. C. Day Lewis, Chatto & Windus,
London 1963.

I went with my friend the doctor Sauvaître to one of the large hospitals one day last week . . . the doctor picked out those needing surgical attention; and these were brought on stretchers to the operating room; formerly a class room, with the familiar inkstains on the floor, walls and ceiling; now a chamber of horrors with blood where ink was. . . . One poor devil had his shin bone crushed by a gun-carriage-wheel and the doctor had to twist it about and push it like a piston to get out the pus. . . . Another had a hole right through the knee. . . . Another had a head into which a ball had entered and come out again. . . . Sometimes the feet were covered with a brown scaly crust— dried blood.

I deliberately tell you all this to educate you to the actualities of the war.[1]

It might reasonably be asked, therefore, what induced Owen to enlist. Not surprisingly, Owen had found encouragement in the work of a poet, the Frenchman, De Vigny. He quotes a passage in a letter to his mother dated June 1915:

. . . 'If any man despairs of becoming a Poet, let him carry his pack and march in the ranks.' Now I don't despair of *becoming* a poet . . . will you set about finding the address of the Artists' Rifles.[2]

In spite of his having seen some of the evils of war, Owen was nonetheless caught up in the wave of war-hysteria which swept Britain at this time, and which appealed to the basic patriotism of all who heard it. Later, when disillusionment set in, Owen was to admit that his initial flush of patriotism was wearing off, but in June 1915 he was fixed in his intention:

I don't want the bore of training, I don't want to wear Khaki; nor yet to save my honour before inquisitive grand-children fifty years hence. But I *now do* most *intensely want to fight*.[3]

By mid-October he had joined the Artists' Rifles, but not before realizing that his patriotism could be swayed by the war's horrors:

[1] *Letters*, p. 284.   [2] *Letters*, p. 342.   [3] *Letters*, p. 341.

> The wounds [of some convalescent soldiers] played the devil
> with my patriotism.[1]

Owen had no strong anti-war beliefs before he enlisted, and, in
fairness to him, it would have been difficult, in the climate of the
times, for him to have lived in England without fighting.

When he first went to France with his regiment, his excitement
at being there after the period of training was enormous. Writing
to his mother on 1 January 1917, he said:

> There is a fine heroic feeling about being in France and I am
> in perfect Spirits.[2]

It is ironic that in the same letter he should recount his first
experience of military action in such exuberant terms:

> This morning I was hit! This morning we were bombing and a
> fragment from somewhere hit my thumb knuckle. I coaxed out
> one drop of blood. Alas! No more!!

Since Owen was shortly to write in letters and poems of the
deadening effect on the senses that seeing all around him through
a film of blood was to have, it is striking that early in the war he
tried to squeeze out more blood from this graze. It shows, of
course, how ready he was to be carried away with what he later
called 'the old lie', that to suffer and die for one's country is a
glorious thing to do.

Disillusionment came rapidly. The joy at being in France and
of facing real action after months of training, the self-satisfaction
of knowing he was playing his part 'for King and Country', soon
became meaningless. He began to put his patriotism into a
perspective and weighed the mass of human suffering and
slaughter against the objectives and gains of the war. He wrote
to his mother on 4 January 1917:

> On all the officers' faces there is a harassed look that I have
> never seen before, and which in England, never will be seen—
> out of jails. The men are . . . expressionless lumps.[3]

It is worth noting, though, that Owen, disillusioned though he
was, still felt quite sure that he was right to be fighting in France.

[1] *Letters*, p. 356.   [2] *Letters*, p. 421.   [3] *Letters*, p. 422.

He was later to describe himself as a 'conscientious objector with a very seared conscience'.[1] This is an extremely revealing remark, indicating as it does Owen's position, finding himself fighting in a war with which he had no convictions, for a side he felt to be no better than his ostensible enemy, and knowing all the time that he ought to be quit of the war and exposing its senseless savagery at home. Yet he did fight on and was at times able to relax into the self-satisfaction of doing what he knew at least *part* of him found acceptable. Thus he could write to his mother on 7 January 1917:

> As I was making my damp bed, I heard the guns for the first time; it was a sound not without a certain sublimity.[2]

and three days later:

> Have no anxiety. I cannot do a better thing or be in a righter place.[3]

As it is true to say that Owen was not *made* a poet by the war, but that the war redirected his poetic gifts and supplied the urgency and subject-matter necessary to utilize his talents, so the war magnified his earliest feelings of dissatisfaction. Very soon his letters show not only a hatred of the war, but a desire to agitate for its end. In the same letter as he described the 'certain sublimity' of the guns, he wrote in passing that:

> I have no Fancies and no Feelings. Positively they went numb with my feet.

By 19 January he was writing, describing his surroundings:

> It is like the eternal place of gnashing of teeth;
> The Slough of Despond could be contained in one of its craters; the first Sodom and Gomorrah would not light a candle to it . . .
> It is pock marked like a body of foulest disease and its odour is the breath of cancer . . .
> The people of England needn't hope. They must agitate. But they are not yet agitated even.[4]

---

[1] *Letters*, p. 423.   [2] *Letters*, p. 423.
[3] *Letters*, p. 427.   [4] *Letters*, p. 429.

From this point on, during the whole of his first spell in France, there is no more reference to the rightness of his situation, only a growing hatred for a war whose origins were by then obscured by the hideous casualty and death lists:

> I can endure cold, and fatigue, and the face-to-face death, as well as another; but extra for me is the universal pervasion of *Ugliness*. Hideous landscapes, vile noises, foul language . . . everything unnatural, broken, blasted; the distortion of the dead, whose unburiable bodies sit outside the dug-outs all day, all night, the most execrable sights on earth. In poetry we call them the most glorious. But to sit with them all day, all night . . . and a week later to come back and find them still sitting there in motionless groups, THAT is what saps the 'soldier's spirit'.[1]

For a man of even ordinary sensitivity to find himself in this situation would have been a shattering experience, but for a man with a highly developed sensitivity such as Owen, the effect must be amplified many times.

The war certainly changed Owen's sense of values and his attitudes to life as dramatically as it altered his poetry:

> . . . I even have to write it down for the sake of future reminders of how incomparable is an innocent and quiet life, at home, of work creative or humdrum, with books or without books, moneyed or moneyless, in sunshine or fog, but under an inoffensive sky, that does not shriek all night with flights of shells.[2]

Owen's attitude to religion changed now too. While always retaining a certain basic belief in the Christian religion, he found the interpretation of Christ's teaching by the established churches to be discordant with what he saw in Christ's message:

> Already I have comprehended a light which will never filter into the dogma of any national church: namely that one of Christ's essential commands was: Passivity at any price! Suffer dishonour and disgrace; but never resort to arms. Be bullied,

---

[1] *Letters*, p. 431.   [2] *Letters*, p. 432.

be outraged, be killed, but do not kill. It may be a chimerical and ignominious principle, but there it is.[1]

This is sharply in contrast to his earlier feelings, but in spite of these views he fought on.

As the war progressed Owen could not maintain the belief that his enemies must be all evil. He saw all soldiers fighting against an even more common enemy—the war itself; its propagators, those who benefited from its continuation; and those who were ignorant of its horrors and who, safe in their home countries, could ensure its continuance. This is the idea expressed by 'The Last Laugh', that *no one* benefits from war. The only laughs come from the weapons, who, being inanimate objects, cannot react with feelings to what is happening, or from the dead who 'smile at nothing, being dead':

Christ is literally in no man's land. There men often hear His voice. Greater love hath no man than this, that he lay down his life—for a friend. Is it spoken in English only and French? I do not believe so.

Thus you see how pure Christianity will not fit in with pure patriotism.[2]

It was shortly after this that Owen was sent back to Britain suffering from shell shock, and it was during his period of recovery that he wrote most of his poems. With the championship of Sassoon; with a vivid experience to draw upon; with a mission to perform—to provide an expressive voice for the 'expressionless lumps'—he turned out most of his poems in a remarkably short space of time. Poetry can hardly be written during a shell or gas attack and Owen needed the tranquillity of Craiglockhart in which to draw on his memory banks. In fact, he only spent two brief periods in the front line, and it was during the second of these that he was killed.

After a year away from the fighting, Owen returned to France in September 1918. Just as on his first going there, when he returned after a year, his memory of the horrors had grown dull. Thus on 1 September 1918, he wrote to his mother:

[1] *Letters*, p. 461.   [2] *Letters*, p. 461.

> Impossible to feel depressed. All auguries are of good fortune.
> How blessedly different from last year.[1]

His optimism, however, was soon destroyed, just as it had been
on the earlier occasion. By October he was writing to Sassoon
that:

> My senses are charred.
> I shall feel again as soon as I dare, but now I must not. I don't
> take the cigarette out of my mouth when I write Deceased over
> their letters. But one day I will write Deceased over many
> books.[2]

Owen was never to have the chance to write poetry again, but
the works he had by then produced have kept his memory alive
throughout the world ever since.

It is probably true that war coarsens the nature of poetry produced during its time. Owen's poems are simple, direct, and
without literary allusions. It is perhaps this non-intellectual
formula which is the keystone of his popularity. The First World
War produced few poets of real standing. Of these, Wilfred Owen
is generally held to be best. Against the back-cloth of the war, art
must have seemed a triviality to many. It is all the more com-
mendable, therefore, that Owen produced what he did.

While we must judge Owen's achievements, not his intentions,
and evaluate him as a poet and not a propagandist, it must be
borne in mind that his poems were given a forced urgency by
his sense of purpose. They are all products designed to provoke
a topical response before it was too late. In October 1918 he
wrote to his mother again:

> I came out in order to help these boys—directly by leading
> them as well as an officer can, indirectly by watching their
> sufferings that I may speak of them as well as a pleader can.
> I have done the first.[3]

Owen was not afraid to be eloquent in pleading what he felt to
be largely a lost cause and he even lapses into the over-precious
and self-consciously 'poetic' at times, but in a controlled way,

[1] *Letters*, p. 572.   [2] *Letters*, p. 581.   [3] *Letters*, p. 580.

tempered with such obvious sincerity, that it cannot be held too highly against him. In his best poems Owen is not self-pitying, but is able to communicate a sympathy which comes from his own participation in what he is writing about, and this endorses his already-made rational claims for peace. The originality and force of his last poems, the passionate nature of his indignation, and his usually controlled style when exposing the horrible 'actualities of the war' are all indications of his ability and success.

There is throughout Owen's poetry a feeling that he wishes to shock readers, but this is only his means of educating his audience. His shockingness comes from the accuracy of his recording what he saw, and his observations are as sharp as they are shocking.

This brings us to a consideration of Owen's technique as a poet. Certainly the writing of his last two years shows that he was serious and self-critical. It can be seen from the many drafts of his later poems that he was continually sharpening his expressions and focusing his language and theme more clearly. Even in his early poetry, a concern for keeping his themes running through an elaborate verse structure is prominent. He was an extremely successful practitioner in verse because of what he was driven to say, but he is not a poetic innovator. The subject of his verse necessitated that people should be shocked out of their lethargy and he was more concerned that they were impressed by what he had to say rather than by how he said it.

Owen's major technical innovation, although he was not its inventor, was his use of half-rhyme, whereby the consonants of a word are kept while the vowels are altered (e.g. boy/buy; foul/foil; paper/piper etc.). This is the opposite of normal rhyme, where the vowel sounds remain the same (e.g. fold/gold; day/may etc.). In Chapter 6 of his book,[1] Dr Welland discusses thoroughly Owen's effective use of a technique which in fact, stretches back through two hundred years of English poets. Here Owen's versification will only be mentioned when it is used to especial effect in particular poems under discussion. It is significant to note, though, that after Owen, many modern poets adopted the half-rhyme technique in their verse. Since one is often tempted to

[1] D. S. R. Welland, *Wilfred Owen A Critical Study*, Chatto & Windus, London 1960.

be highly critical of the precious nature of parts of his work, it is good to find an area in which he was positively progressive.

When Owen recorded that his intention was 'to help these boys' and said that as a leader he had helped them in one way, he was understating his own success. Owen the fighting soldier and officer is forgotten, but Owen the poet has his effect to this day.

Owen and the other 'War Poets'

The classification 'war poets' is usually applied to Owen and Sassoon primarily, with Rosenberg and Graves as minor members of this group. Strangely, though quite different in attitude and much more conventional in technique, Rupert Brooke is also included. In looking at Owen alongside these other 'war poets', it might be suitable to deal with Brooke first, since the contrast between him and Owen is most obvious.

Rupert Brooke

Rupert Brooke is really rather inaptly thought of as a 'war poet' since he never saw the war at first hand. He died in 1914 before he could reach the fighting front, and the number of his poems which have war as their subject is very few. What has made Brooke noteworthy is his strongly patriotic attitude. His patriotism was blindly loyal and of the sort that believed in the nobility of dying for one's country. The famous lines from his poem 'The Soldier' show this:

> If I should die, think only this of me:
> That there's some corner of a foreign field
> That is for ever England. . . .

He believed that the loss of life and the pain and suffering of the war are all acceptable because God is on his side, and what is life to an everlasting reward?

> In hearts at peace, under an English heaven.

In his poem 'The Dead' the same sentiments again appear:

> . . . He leaves a white
> Unbroken glory, a gathered radiance,
> A width, a shining peace, under the night.

Brooke's Christian optimism was not shared by many who knew
the real horrors of the war. For him the pain was the instantaneous
agony of death, not the agony of living with destroyed lungs or
without limbs, or of total mental breakdown. The blood that so
incapacitated Owen's senses, for Brooke is 'the red sweet wine of
youth'—easily given up. Consider the following poem:

The Dead

Blow out, you bugles, over the rich Dead!
There's none of these so lonely and poor of old,
But, dying, has made us rarer gifts than gold.
These laid the world away; poured out the red
Sweet wine of youth; gave up the years to be
Of work and joy, and that unhoped serene,
That men call age; and those who would have been,
Their sons, they gave, their immortality.

Blow, bugles blow! They brought us, for our dearth,
Holiness, lacked so long, and Love, and Pain.
Honour has come back, as a king, to earth,
And paid his subjects with a royal wage;
And Nobleness walks in our ways again;
And we have come into our heritage.

Contrast this with Owen's 'Anthem for Doomed Youth', which
also opens with clamorous noise, but it is the knell of the guns,
and which ends not with glorious—though meaningless—expressions of achievement, but with a slow drawing down of
blinds. Brooke's poems are stuffed with concepts which were
quite meaningless to the fighting soldier, and indeed, as used by
Brooke, are meaningless to any ordinary reader: Holiness,
Honour, Nobleness, Heritage. Instead of acknowledging that
between 1914 and 1918 the world was entering one of its blackest
periods, Brooke sees it as coming into the fruits of the centuries
which, like the 'gifts' of the personified Kingly Honour, are
actually horror and brutality on a quite unprecedented scale.

Brooke is read now with a sense of embarrassment by everyone,
even the most patriotic. Few would accept his assurance of the

total rightness of the British side in the war. Quite certainly, no one would see the bloodshed of the war justified by his notion that it brought new vigour and masculinity into a decadent Pre-War Europe.

> Glad from a world grown old and cold and weary,
> Leave the sick hearts that honour could not move,
> And half-men, and their dirty songs and dreary,
> And all the little emptiness of love!

In their viewpoints on the war, Owen and Brooke are obviously poles apart, but less obviously they are distanced in their techniques. Owen, though not a great innovator, still made use of the unusual device of half-rhyme, and even with the more conventional technique of alliteration he created striking effects. He was generally more forward-looking than Brooke, whose entirely 'Georgian' poetry suffers from all the worst defects of that staid style of verse.

Robert Graves

Robert Graves was one of the poets who survived the First World War, but as he wrote in the foreword to his *Collected Poems*, it 'permanently changed my outlook on life'. Though he wrote very few poems about the war or military life, those he did write are effective mainly through his employment of scornful and ironic invective. Consider his poem 'Recalling War' aimed against the idea that the war would bring chivalry back to a sordid world. Here, the weapons are spoken of in the tone often used by Owen, making them seem toys (cf. 'The Last Laugh')—but deadly toys put into the hands of irresponsible children.

Graves caught his attitude to the war in a very effective simile:

> As when the morning traveller turns and views
> His wild night-stumbling carved into a hill.[1]

This is not a picture of spiritual vigour in a new age, but of frantic and fatal errors.

> Natural infirmities were out of mode,
> For Death was young again; patron alone
> Of healthy dying, premature fate-spasm.

[1] Robert Graves, *Collected Poems*, Cassell & Co, London 1959.

In what may be an indirect reference to the sickly poetry of
Brooke, Graves states:

> Never was such antiqueness of romance.
> Such tasty honey oozing from the heart.

By comparison, Brooke's poetry is oozing in its comfortable
assurance.

> Even there was a use again for God—

On a larger scale, Graves, like Owen, saw the war as horrific
and totally destructive. The very antithesis of Brooke's belief that
Europe had come into her heritage is expressed by Graves:

> War was return of earth to ugly earth,
> War was foundering of sublimities,
> Extinction of each happy art and faith
> By which the world had still kept head in air.

Graves differs from Owen in that he writes about war from
the distance of many years and does not recall the details of the
soldiers' lives. His impact comes more from the objective verdict
which he expresses:

> And we recall the merry ways of guns—
> Nibbling the walls of factory and church
> Like a child, piecrust; felling groves of trees
> Like a child, dandelions with a switch.
> Machine-guns rattle toy-like from a hill,
> Down in a row the brave tin-soldiers fall.

Owen had a somewhat similar tone in a few of his poems, and
though he would have been describing the last gasps of the 'tin-
soldiers' as they died, he would have shared Graves' condemnation
of the irresponsible perpetuation of the war in the hands of statesmen who were as ignorant of the real conditions as the innocently
destructive children of the poem above.

From a technical point of view, Graves is much more advanced
than Owen. But he wrote the poem just quoted some twenty
years after the war. Generally, the tone of his poetry is more
ironic, even sarcastic, than Owen's, whose attempts at irony,
under the influence of Sassoon, for example, produced an

unconvincing effect. Graves' diction, too, is sharper and less obviously 'poetic' than Owen's, but their opinions on the war are identical.

Isaac Rosenberg

The same cannot entirely be said of Isaac Rosenberg, a poet three years older than Owen who was killed in action in the same year. Rosenberg's output is small but very fine. His poetry sprang from the simultaneous attraction and repulsion which he felt about the war. This complexity provides a deeper interest in him than in other poets of the time whose attitudes, though vehement and unquestionably genuine, were of a simpler, more straightforward nature.

In his poem 'Marching' there is a certain fascination expressed for the 'walls' of soldiers he sees in front of him; their power at once appeals to and appalls him:

> We husband the ancient glory
> In these bared necks and hands
> Nor broke is the forge of Mars;

Yet it is his sense of the futility of militarism and its inevitable self-destruction which has the last word in the poem:

> Blind fingers loose an iron cloud
> To rain immortal darkness
> On strong eyes.

Again, in 'August, 1914', the richness is taken from life and the iron alone left:

> Three lives hath one life—
> Iron, honey, gold.
> The gold and honey gone—
> Left is the hard and cold.

In his poems that deal with trench life, Rosenberg, unlike Owen, has an almost detached view of his situation, mentioning the presence of the dirt and squalor and vermin, but dwelling on the fate of a rat—as in 'Break of Day in the Trenches'. In this poem, the action of plucking a poppy and sticking it behind his ear while surrounded by 'The torn fields of France' seems to symbolize the madness which so many thinking men found in their situation during the war.

The Rosenberg poem nearest to Owen in content and tone is 'Dead Man's Camp'.

> The wheels lurched over sprawled dead
> But pained them not, though their bones crunched,
> Their shut mouths made no moan.

Here we have the vivid reporting quality of Owen, combined with the same power to evoke the sense of waste and vain squalor of the war, and also the feeling of personal futility in the face of this self-perpetuating monster. What Rosenberg does not have, though, is Owen's sense of sympathy for, and identification with, the suffering of the men. Rosenberg's horrifying fascination is brought out at times here, too:

> Maniac Earth! howling and flying, your bowels
> Seared by the jagged fire, the iron love,
> The impetuous storm of savage love.

The 'savage love' image is a curious one, illustrating the strangely ambivalent attitude of fascination/repulsion which Rosenberg felt so strongly within him. The whole of this poem concentrates more entirely on the blandness with which Rosenberg can face the awful destruction which surrounds him—rather in the way that Owen claims he can look at the bloodshed from seeing his whole world through a filter of blood. Rosenberg is looking at himself and is as much disgusted with what he sees there as with what he sees all round him.

Technically, Rosenberg is more adventurous and up-to-date than Owen, although this does not make him superior, and in some ways his more introspective and abstract views on the war now have greater appeal. Certainly, had he lived, Rosenberg would have been an extremely interesting poet.

Siegfried Sassoon

This brings us finally to Siegfried Sassoon. Sassoon survived the war, of course, and so was able to write of it in later years with the advantage of retrospect. Even so, the poems which he wrote during the war are characterized by an all-pervading bitterness against its continuance. He had entered the war willingly, but as with Owen, this feeling soon wore off. He wrote:

> I believe that this war, upon which I entered as a war of defence and liberation, has now become a war of aggression and conquest.

His disillusionment shows itself most forcibly in the enormous indignation which he displays in his poetry—mainly by employing a cynical, sarcastic tone throughout. Like Owen, he could report with frightening accuracy the sordid details of life which he observed:

> Dim, gradual thinning of the shapeless gloom
> Shudders to drizzling daybreak, that reveals
> Disconsolate men who stamp their sodden boots
> And turn dulled, sunken faces to the sky
> Haggard and hopeless. . . .

Sassoon shows no lack of understanding of the conditions in the trenches, where 'nothing blossoms but the sky', but again there is not the same power to create real pathos that Owen has. Sassoon's poetry has all the indications of stemming from actual experience and all the strength of violent indignation, but no more. He was an accomplished poet technically, though, and careful polishing is evident in his work. His versification is at much the same level as Owen's—he also makes much use of alliteration and personification and creates a sensation of the futility of the war by referring to his fellow soldiers as 'the dead', thereby stressing the inevitability of their deaths:

> I stood with the dead. . . . They were dead; they
>   were dead:

Sassoon's chief poetic device is irony. The line just quoted displays this, as do others in the same poem, 'I Stood With the Dead':

> My heart and my head beat a march of dismay:
> And gusts of the wind came dulled by the guns.
> 'Fall in!' I shouted; 'Fall in for your pay!'

The reader is left in no doubt as to the real nature of the soldiers' pay—maiming and death.

Though the two were close friends, and Owen relied on Sassoon's judgement, Sassoon did not influence Owen's poetry very much. Owen's attempts at direct speech, usually for ironic effect, often do not quite come off. The speech usually does not fit the character concerned and shatters the tone and effect of the poem. Owen's elegiac, rather lofty style does not mix with the colloquial or the ironic, and he was keen-sighted enough to realize this. Thus, while Sassoon shares his indignation, his visual accuracy and his sense of craftsmanship, he lacks the sense of exultation which figures in many of Owen's best poems. It is obvious that both felt deeply concerned for their men, but Sassoon does not seem to identify totally with them in the same way.

The purpose of this brief comparison between Owen and the other First World War poets is not an attempt to prove Owen a better poet than the others, it is merely to give an outline of their various approaches. Clearly some were more technically competent and some more intellectual in their range of allusion than Owen, but each was trying in his own way to bring about the same effect. Owen is certainly the most popular of these war poets today, and this can only be ascribed to his capacity, which the other lack, for making his reader enter the trenches with the soldiers. Reading Owen, anyone can understand and join with the most ordinary soldier in his predicament.

The War Poems

Preface

The Preface to Owen's war poems which is printed in all the editions of his poetry is often misleading. It was an unfinished sketch, and so it is not reliable to treat it as an expression of his thought-out ideas. His main point is that he does not intend to glorify the war, but to provide a memorial to all those who have died by putting forward a plea for those still fighting. His poetry is not consolation, it is rebuke and warning.

> Above all I am not concerned with Poetry.
> My subject is War, and the pity of War.
> The Poetry is in the pity.

What Owen is saying in these lines is apparent in his poems; that he is writing for a purpose—the ending of the war—for which the self-conscious type of Pre-Raphaelite, sentimental poetry is useless. It is a warning to those who might look for an emotional escape in his work.

The danger of reading too much into this sketched preface is clear. The wrong meaning, too often assumed, is that Owen is claiming no interest in his poetry, only in its effect. This is simply not so. He was certainly expressing a point of view, but he was always aware that he was doing so within the discipline of verse, and his manuscripts show that he was as thorough in working at these war poems as he was on any before the war.

Strange Meeting

This is one of Owen's most unusual and effective poems. Though it has some clumsy lines and expressions, it has a haunting

quality which few of his other poems possess. After death, the
narrator meets an apparent enemy whom he has killed, and in
him finds a friend who shares his hatred of the whole business of
the war.

The dreamlike tone of the poem is evoked by the first words,
'It seemed . . .', and continued throughout the first ten lines.
Though these lines are descriptive of the place and atmosphere
in which the narrator finds himself, Owen also uses them to
imply a concept which occurs throughout his poems: that finding
oneself in hell is a release after the battlefields:

> And by his smile, I knew that sullen hall,
> By his dead smile I knew we stood in Hell.

The association of the traditional Christian notion of hell as a
place of eternal torment tacitly leaves the reader with the conclusion that if hell is to be smiled through, the trenches and
battlefields must have been places of incomparable horror. Owen
creates this effect, however, by a sort of negative deduction on
the part of his reader. The same point is endorsed in the following
few lines:

> With a thousand pains that vision's face was grained;
> Yet no blood reached there from the upper ground,
> And no guns thumped, or down the flues made moan.

Among the sleepers in this hell, the narrator is confronted by
one who stares 'with piteous recognition' at him. This stranger
then lists the various causes for his mourning: 'the undone
years/the hopelessness' and, more significantly, the fact that he
has not had the opportunity to tell the truth about the war. At
this point Owen introduces another idea into the poem, that this
strange friend is apparently the narrator's direct counterpart on
the enemy side. Owen believed that the war had somehow
developed a momentum of its own and, like Sassoon, felt that
whatever principles may have lain behind its beginning had been
forgotten. The war was by then a separate entity and so the
soldiers in it were in no real sense enemies, but mutual victims
of the gathering, crushing impetus of events. Owen, along with
many soldiers, felt a growing lack of hatred for his adversaries
who he realized were as helpless in their situation as he was in

his. This theme is brought out all through the poem, not merely in the forgiveness of the last lines but in the statement of the similar feelings which both men possess. By creating a character who is *called* an enemy but who is identical in spirit, Owen appears to be illustrating two sides of one personality and showing how the tag 'enemy' does not have any validity when applied to men facing the common threat of a war which is somehow bigger than the total mass of all engaged in it.

The friend's list of regrets at being no longer part of life divides into two distinct areas: one dealing with the sense of personal loss, the loss of pleasures and sensations; the other dealing with the loss of the opportunity to warn the world of its course towards chaos.

> . . . I went hunting wild
> After the wildest beauty in the world,
> Which lies not calm in eyes, or braided hair,
> But mocks the steady running of the hour,

But his main concern is for

> . . . the truth untold
> The pity of war, the pity war distilled.

The sense of loss is perfectly captured in the lines:

> Now men will go content with what we spoiled,
> Or, discontent, boil bloody, and be spilled.
> They will be swift with the swiftness of the tigress.
> None will break ranks, though nations trek from
> progress.

All the world is distorted and destroyed and blindly moving away from advancement. To add double effect, no one, he claims, will notice; the expressions 'break ranks' and 'trek' suggest an army marching reluctantly in a drilled fashion, unthinkingly accepting the marred remains of life. The real sense of loss, however, comes when the friend expresses his regret at not having had the chance to use the courage, ability, and wisdom which he had, to warn and to repair some of the war's damage.

> Courage was mine, and I had mystery,
> Wisdom was mine, and I had mastery:

> To miss the march of this retreating world
> Into vain citadels that are not walled.

The idea is striking, for it implies that the military attitude struck by the various nations is the cause of the retreat, and simultaneously suggests the rapid pace with which this retreat is being put into effect. The citadels without walls can either apply to the metaphorical mental bastions of national prejudice and aggression or can be emphasizing the folly of any nation's thinking it can maintain an impregnable position in a modern war. The final word on war is to call it a 'cess'. Given a full life, the friend would have used 'truths that lie too deep for taint' as healing.

The complete lack of resentment in the statement

> I am the enemy you killed, my friend.

with the contrast between the conventional tag 'enemy' and the personal expression 'my friend' serves to amplify the impression of futility behind the situation. The lack of hatred for his killer is made to seem almost an expression of thanks, for bringing relief from the hell of life in the trenches—and so we are brought back to the first notion of the poem; and with the invitation to sleep in the last line we are carried back to the dreamlike beginning.

This poem has a few lines which one might grumble over: 'Through granites which titanic wars had groined' for example, seems to be rather too orientated towards sound alone. Some words, too, we might feel are rather precious: 'richlier' or the phrase 'down the flues', which seems rather banal in the context. But on the whole 'Strange Meeting' makes a complex plea for a renewed look at the war. The bizarre theme is an imaginative stroke seldom repeated by Owen.

Insensibility

This is a poem in which a sense of fatality and great bitterness is linked with deep sympathy and expansive vision.

To understand at least part of Owen's statement in this poem, we must realize that it is representative of the resentment felt by many of the men fighting at the front towards the politicians at home who prolonged the war, and towards those who, safely out of danger, were unconcerned at its continuance. His attack is one of the most direct and forceful of the kind he ever made. But this is a wide-ranging poem which touches on many other topics in its six sections.

The very first line of the poem creates an air of fatality which is continued throughout:

> Happy are men who yet before they are killed

There is no hope extended here. All who are there will die, claims Owen. Any happiness they may have is in the contorted pleasure of becoming immune to what is going on around them. Owen uses irony to great effect by adopting the tone of the Beatitudes of St Matthew's Gospel but in reverse. Thus he states that it is blessed to have the very opposite qualities to those which Christ extolled, and which we know to be humanly desirable, and shows that in the situation of the war they are of great benefit. The effect upon the reader is to stress the total distortion by war of the good and bad aspects of life. Those who are lucky in these circumstances are the hard-hearted; those whose imaginations either never have been active or have been dulled by the war. Blessed are the oblivious and the ignorant who feel no ambition and correspondingly no loss more acute than the loss of life— which is stressed as their common fate throughout. Blessed are those with little sense of the fullness of life, for their loss likewise is less than in those of wider experience. Cursed, however, are those who by choice remain unmoved by what they know to be happening but by which they are unaffected.

The first section deals with those who 'Can let their veins run cold'. Deadened to normal feelings, they need not assume the mockery of a show of compassion. The use of 'fleers' is perhaps rather quaint, but by nature of its very sound, it includes 'fears' and 'leers'—both of which overtones accord with the actual meanings of the word itself. The word 'cobbled' in the next line not only suggests the total deadness of the other troops, but indicates their numbers and also reflects the feelings of those who walk on them, with as much thought for them as for the cobbles on a road. This is Owen using words and their connotations to

supreme effect. The first section seems at first sight rather disjointed, for in the middle lines Owen leaves the hard-hearted and
deals with the dead themselves. In the last line, however, he effects
a unity with the beginning by the line '. . . but no one bothers',
which brings the reader back to the hard-heartedness of the
beginning. The loss of soldiers is like the withering of flowers,
regretted, but only fleetingly; they cause gaps which must be
filled and replacements are ever available. In passing, Owen
tries to assert a note of reality into the situation:

> But they are troops who fade, not flowers
> For poets' tearful fooling:
> Men. . . .

but again the atmosphere of insensibility returns for the rest of
the section till the final '. . . but no one bothers'. As a poet,
Owen was doing all he could to plead, but the note of regret at
what must inevitably have appeared to him as only 'tearful
fooling' is a pathetic reminder of how trapped he himself was.

The second section mentions the men who have lost any feelings
for themselves as well as for other people. They feel no anxiety
in their position because they resign themselves to fate:

> Dullness best solves
> The tease and doubt of shelling,

The word 'tease' has a double meaning here. To the numbed
men, devoid of all senses, including fear, the shelling is no more
than a petty annoyance. But 'tease' can also mean 'to pull apart',
as in teasing fibres. Thus Owen uses it to convey simultaneously
the destructive nature of the shelling and the insignificance of it
to the insensible soldiers. The reference to the shilling is, of course,
to the money paid to every soldier when they enlisted, and Owen
offsets it against the 'armies' decimation' to imply the cheap and
continuous availability of soldiers to replace the gaps as armies are
wiped out by a tenth of their strength at a time.

Section III reverts to the ironic vein again. Imagination is
better left behind, it is a burden to be carried like a heavy pack.
Once the imagination is gone, all horrors can be looked on with
equanimity. In the lines

> Having seen all things red,
> Their eyes are rid
> Of the hurt of the colour of blood forever.

Owen explains a sensation which he alludes to elsewhere in his work. Just as a coloured filter in a light causes everything to be seen in that colour of light and so deprives objects of the same colour of any distinctive effect, so the continual sight of blood diminishes the effect it might at one time have had. Similarly, once real terror has 'constricted' the heart, it never again expands to its full emotional awareness. Owen is, of course, using poetic diction here in referring to the heart, but we know that he means the senses generally, for once they are seared, as the last three lines say, a callousness—and cauterization quite literally means hardening of the skin into callouses—follows.

Section IV deals with the innocent soldiers who, before they are exposed to the war, are not afraid, for fear comes from experience. As was shown in the Introduction to this book, Owen himself had in fact been in such a state while in England so he knew what an impact the transition between training in Britain and life in the trenches could bring about. The contrast between the ordinary soldier, the 'lad whose mind was never trained' who 'sings along the march' and the men who know action, who 'march taciturn', silent because they know there is no escape, is enforced painfully. The pessimism is all pervading:

> The long, forlorn, relentless trend
> From larger day to huger night.

Section V contrasts with the ordinary soldier of the previous section by dealing with the conscious, thinking man involved in the war. But there is no condescension extended towards the ordinary soldier. Both he and the thinking man are caught up in a terrible common experience, and here Owen is attempting to view the war as a new recruit might see it 'through his blunt and lashless eyes'. The result is a picture of inertia and resignation:

> Alive, he is not vital overmuch;
> Dying, not mortal overmuch;
> Nor sad, nor proud,
> Nor curious at all.

He is resigned, docile, inactive—insensible.

> He cannot tell
> Old men's placidity from his.

Owen breaks the slow, exhausted tone of Section V by launching into violent reproach at the beginning of the last section:

> But cursed are dullards whom no cannon stuns,

The rapid movement of the line with 'cursed' awakens the reader to Owen's final pronouncement against the dullness not of the battered, shell-shocked troops, but of those who are deliberately insensible to the suffering of the soldiers; those who are safe and so unconcerned. Their poverty of spirit is not that of the man whose senses have been crushed by battle; their ignorance is not the naïvity of the raw recruits:

> By choice they made themselves immune
> To pity and whatever mourns in man

And yet the poem ends by showing that though they may not suffer, Owen's curse is not entirely without effect, for they are excluded from real human contact; they are unable to share in the deepest human emotions; they cannot sympathize with the suffering. By their hard-heartedness they are cut off from their fellow men, excluded from

> The eternal reciprocity of tears.

This is a truly great war poem—possibly Owen's finest. His language is always vital and he uses half-rhyme to effect, causing just enough jarring to make us notice the meanings of these words more carefully. He explores a whole field of human reaction with a vision and sympathy that are seldom bettered. As anti-war propaganda it is immediate in its impact, while as poetry alone it can bear up to the closest critical scrutiny and rank with any poem on this subject.

Apologia Pro Poemate Meo

This poem goes one step further than 'Insensibility' and excludes the reader from a proper understanding of the subject of the poem. We may understand what Owen is saying but, he claims, we will never comprehend the strange beauty which he has seen in even the most hideous circumstances. Such vision is for those who experience these events, not for those who merely read of them.

> Nevertheless, except you share
> With them in hell the sorrowful dark of hell,
> . . . You shall not hear their mirth:

Far from daunting the reader, however, this paradoxical approach makes one more willing to enter fully into the spirit of the poem and to try to see what Owen found in the trenches that he believes we will not understand.

An apologia is a reasoned defence of the conduct or opinions of the writer, and here Owen is trying to extend several lines of justification for his work. First, as we know, he is trying to show the war's horrors in shocking detail, thereby defending his anti-war opinions. Second, he is anxious to arouse his readers from the torpor of their complacent acceptance of the war: he wanted people to work for its ending. Finally, like any poet, he wishes to show how he sees more in the situation in which he is than most ordinary men have found: a strange beauty; a friendship deeper than would be possible elsewhere; even a source of amusement and exultation where they would little be expected. It is necessary that a poet records these, for this, as well as his more expedient reasons, is a real justification for writing poetry on such a subject and under such conditions. He is almost saying that anyone can plead for the war's cessation, but that few could comprehend so much variety in this situation. As such, this is a perfectly planned apologia in which the sense of being excluded compels the reader into a more determined effort to follow him, thereby securing the poem's double effect.

The poem relies heavily on the effect of irony and paradox throughout. We do not expect to hear of the men in the trenches smiling, yet Owen records that they do, while all the time stressing the squalor of the situation. It is 'wretches' who laugh, and their laughter becomes the laughter of hysteria as they are caught up in a frenzy of unfeeling actions:

> Merry it was to laugh there—
> Where death becomes absurd and life absurder.
> For power was on us as we slashed bones bare
> Not to feel sickness or remorse of murder.

He goes on to register the events which have had a strange attraction for him: the occasional chance to permit his imagination to soar 'Past the entanglement where hopes lay strewn'; the elation of having led his men safely, and at the sight of the gratitude on their faces, and the companionship that caring for one another's wounds can create—a form of love deeper, he claims, than conventional lovers' experience.

> For love is not the binding of fair lips
> With the soft silk of eyes that look and long,

In the midst of soldiers' curses, which, though apparently foul, served to keep their spirits up, he has found beauty. In the silence of being alone at his post, he has experienced happiness. In the midst of the worst and most destructive shelling, he has found tranquillity. All these are obviously paradoxical notions, and Owen leaves us to ponder them by breaking into a reproach to those who may be interested in the nature of this odd beauty, reproving those who may not understand these sensations by repeating that unless they are in the situation they will never apprehend his meaning. The poem ends with a note of bitterness:

> . . . These men are worth
> Your tears. You are not worth their merriment.

This is a poem of subtle effect. Its basic technique of presenting a baffling series of insights and then, rather than explaining them, accusing and excluding the reader by insisting that to share these feelings he should be *with* the troops, not reading *of* them, is a highly sophisticated move on Owen's part. What begins as an apologia thus ends as a diatribe and the dual effect is achieved.

Greater Love

After the three great poems discussed above we come to one of Owen's less successful ventures, for 'Greater Love' is a poem of uneven quality. It compares the nature of patriotic love and of sensual physical love. The title is an allusion to Christ's pronouncement: Greater love hath no man than this, that he lay down his life for a friend. The patriotic love of Owen is not foolishly romanticized like Brooke's, but in contrast to physical love it appears in Owen's view as a highly superior emotion. Having outlined this general theme, Owen's technique is to select certain conventional lovers' clichés and comparisons—the red lips, the attractive eyes, the soft voice, etc.—and to show that by giving up their lives for their friends and their country, the soldiers are exhibiting a nobler form of love, before which the physical enticements seem weak and sordid.

The first stanza of this poem is probably the best. Owen takes the redness of a woman's lips as a somewhat usual point of contrast to the redness of the blood of the dead soldiers who kiss only the stones as they fall dead upon them. This image of the chaste love of the soldier is extended to contrast with even the most harmless of lover's exchanges, the 'kindness of wooed and wooer' which by comparison 'seems shame to their love pure'. Finally, Owen claims that even a lover's eyes lose enticement when he looks on a soldier's sightless eyes and thinks that he might have suffered that fate.

The second stanza continues this theme but this time Owen brings out one contrast only and the image of pure and profane love is developed further by comparing a wounded soldier rolling in agony to lovers rolling in sexual ecstasy. As lovers would become more and more physically involved up to a final climax, so the stabbed soldier is gripped with a sort of ecstasy until the final climax, which for him is death.

> Rolling and rolling there
> Where God seems not to care;
> Till the fierce love they bear
> Cramps them in death's extreme decrepitude.

The image of sexual love is only broken at the word 'Cramps'. As in sex so in death, the experience is a wearing one (suggested here by 'decrepitude') but the main difference is that while sex gives a feeling of relief, death brings the harsh experience of cramp. It would probably be crediting Owen with too much to

assume that by contrasting love and death in this way, he is
referring to the seventeenth-century literary convention of pun-
ning dying to mean both physical death and also the state of
relaxation immediately following sex. Owen's reading, we know,
was not sufficiently extensive for us to be sure that he would be
aware of this literary practice, for the metaphysical poets who
most used this form of word-play were only just coming back into
fashion by the time of his death.

Stanzas three and four are noticeably weaker than the first
two. The comparison between the commonplace expressions of
female beauty is protracted here still, but the approach is
beginning to wear thin. To say that the voice of the girl is not as
precious as the voice that those now dead once possessed is really
not very effective in itself, but coupled with the ugly line

> Now earth has stopped their piteous mouths that
> coughed.

the stanza loses all impact. Much the same must also be said of
the last stanza. To say that no lover's heart was ever as full as
a soldier's heart when it has just stopped a bullet is patently
absurd.

> Heart, you were never hot
> Nor large, nor full like hearts made great with shot;

The rest of the stanza likewise simply does not make sense as it
is written.

> And though your hand be pale,

The 'your' appears to refer to the heart which he has used as an
image by which he can personify the lover, and if this is so what
of the 'hand'? Can a heart have hands? And does the cross of
the penultimate line refer to the heart too, and if so what does it
mean? Does it mean that lovers and loving affections and
memories are merely burdens? Owen does not make this at all
clear. The last line is ambiguous, too, for it appears that Owen
cannot decide on the tone to adopt in it. Is he being scornful at
the lovers who may weep but cannot help at all? Is he gloating
that no one can despoil the purity of the men who kissed the
ground only? Certainly the implications of the ending of this

poem are numerous—the tone is almost unavoidably misogynistic and, although he may not have intended it, one feels that Owen has been so anxious to show the immaculate nature of the sacrifice and 'greater love' of his men that he is now glad they are safely dead and away from corruption.

So this is a flawed poem which begins interestingly but loses impact as the sharpness of Owen's focus is lost. As it becomes more ambiguous, so the theme of lovers and soldiers alone is not enough to support it and the reader is confused and even bewildered by it. One interesting point is the exploitation by Owen of half-rhyme, but again, because the poem generally loses impetus, this technique also ceases to have effect.

The Parable of the Old Man and the Young

This is a short allegorical poem in which Owen adapts and modifies the story of Abraham's near sacrifice of his son, as told in the Bible in Genesis, Chapter 22. It must be noted that Owen modifies the story considerably, for in the Bible Abraham goes through the motions of preparing the sacrifice with great reluctance and is only too glad to spare his son in favour of a ram when the purpose of the sacrifice—to test Abraham's faith —is over. In the poem, the old man appears to act out of mere cruelty and when given the chance of avoiding the killing of his son, quite deliberately ignores it. Apart from the mention of parapets and trenches in line 8 (and possibly belts and straps, with their military overtones, in the previous line), there is no indication given that this is anything other than a rephrasing of the biblical account. The allegory clearly veils the heads of state in the various warring nations under the guise of Abraham, and the son, as the last line indicates, is 'half the seed of Europe'. The 'Ram of Pride' is what Owen sees as the cause of the war, national pride and supposed supremacy. What he stresses is the calculating way in which the nations gathered their weapons together and prepared for this sacrifice, and even when offered a chance of drawing back, chose to go on with the slaughter.

This short poem does not make a great impact, mainly because the allegory is used only to convey the one point made in the last three lines. To be effective, a parable must really bring together a simple or well-known story and a new situation which is to be seen in the light of the initial tale, and they must coincide on as many points as possible.

Arms and the Boy

This is another simple poem which, like the one before, makes little real effect upon its readers. A young boy, probably a recruit whom Owen has seen, who seems particularly unsuited for war and noticeably unaware of what he is entering upon, is invited to look more closely at weapons while Owen outlines their real nature to him.

The bayonet blade is made to seem like a carnivorous animal, vicious by nature and thin because hungry to devour human prey. The first stanza, although not exceptional, is spoiled by one half-line which, as far as can be seen, has no meaning at all, and that is 'like a madman's flash'. What exactly is 'a madman's flash'? It is no use approaching Owen's poetry blindly and saying that we can take a suggested meaning from the isolated words 'madman' and 'flash', both of which have connotations of their own. We must seriously probe his imagery, and here the simile is simply a waste of time, for it can convey no added depth of understanding since none of his readers can find sense in it. This is an example of one of Owen's greatest faults, sound controlling sense, instead of assisting it as in 'Insensibility'.

Stanza two opens with an archaic use of 'lend', meaning 'help', which we can only assume is used alliteratively, but the sound of the l's is too broken up with the intervening four words before 'blind' to create much effect. Here Owen uses 'nuzzle' referring to the bullets, but while a bullet fired at the boy may have a lead 'nose', it would hardly 'nuzzle' its way into his heart as Owen claims. It would bore or shatter or smash or any word with violent overtones. The biting cartridges are more accurately personified as having teeth, but Owen does nothing to emphasize this notion by linking it to the worn-out image:

Sharp with the sharpness of grief and death.

In the final stanza, the boy himself is touched upon. He is no bird of prey or fighting stag. He is made for laughter and happiness, not for war. Owen comes near to pathos by simply describing the ingenuous pleasantness of the lad. He has fine teeth and thick curls, and yet we know that his presence in battle means certain death. There is a strong similarity in tone here, and elsewhere in Owen's work, with A. E. Housman's *The Shropshire Lad*. Housman's country lads are all inevitably sporting heads of fine teeth and curls, and about them there is often an air of fatality. The similarities might be explored further, but that would be beyond the scope of this book. It is very likely, however, that Owen knew these poems, which were published in 1896—their popularity at a time when Owen was anxious to be a 'poet' must have caused him to read them—and quite possible that their simple style appealed to him.

Regardless of Housman's influence—if indeed it does exist—this poem makes little impression on the reader. It is a weak attempt at the sort of personification which is effective in 'The Last Laugh', but in that poem the violence of the images and the tenser subject brings the imagery alive. The only effect of 'Arms and the Boy' is a passing feeling of sadness.

Anthem for Doomed Youth

One of Owen's most famous poems, this sonnet continues the basic theme of 'Greater Love' by dwelling on the soldiers' sacrifice and echoing its purity in the form of remembrance they deserve. By calling the poem an anthem, Owen is trying to convey a sense of its seriousness. He might have written 'Hymn . . .' but that would not have reflected the formality of a choir piece that he wishes to evoke. Though the choirs are 'choirs of wailing shells', the poem itself, especially in the last six lines (the sestet, as it is known), has a grandness of tone fitting such a ceremonious occasion.[1] The title is worth considering further, for the phrase 'Doomed Youth' broadens the poem's range of application. It is not just for those already dead, but to all of youth whom Owen

[1] This poem, and 'Futility' are both very effectively set to music as part of Britten's *War Requiem*.

sees as being in such danger. As was clear in 'Strange Meeting', one of his main purposes was to warn as many people as he could of the war's horrors and how engulfing they could become. Those to whom this poem is addressed are not yet dead, but they are threatened, and though, in his pessimistic way, Owen sees them as already doomed, he still gives out this warning.

The sonnet falls into two sections, octave and sestet. In the former, Owen presents a noisy requiem for the thousands of dead, and in the latter part he adopts a more sombre note as he thinks of those who, in conscious and subconscious ways, will remember the dead.

The first line gives a curiously detached tone to the poem with the word 'these'. The impersonality is deliberately created, for, as we see in the same line, the men die in vast herds, like cattle. Since there is no thought given to them on the battlefield, why should Owen present a different view in his poem? The notion of the men dying as cattle is a jarring one and deliberately used to shock his readers into a greater awareness of the total carnage of the war. This was not a chivalrous gentleman's war, it was a war in which mechanized weapons mowed men down in columns and Owen is determined that none of this escapes his reader. Thus he asks the rhetorical question:

> What passing-bells for these who die as cattle?

The mockery in the tone of the line, conveyed by the idea of ringing a solemn knell for slaughtered beasts, is also for the same effect. This is altogether one of the most arresting and challenging lines in all of Owen's work.

In the second line we hear an ironic response to the first line's question, that the only mourners are the very instruments of destruction, the angry guns. Similarly, in lines 3 and 4 the rifles rap out quick prayers—for those they have just killed! The alliteration in line 3 is obvious, of course, but none the less effective, adding as it does a dimension of sound to the meaning already in the line:

> Only the stuttering *r*ifles' *r*apid *r*attle

This alliterative sound is carried on into the next line, too, with the t's of 'patter' echoing the t's of 'rattle'. Line 4, however, is

also interesting for an extremely adroit pun. The meaning of the
line is that the guns will rap out prayers for the dead—and it is
ironic that by so doing they will be shooting at other soldiers
and offering them simultaneous prayers and death—and the
sound of the guns will be a quick 'patter'. 'Patter' itself has
harmless overtones and sounds too innocent for its deadly nature,
but it is also the word applied to glib, rapidly repeated prayers,
and more significantly, it is the obsolete name for The Lord's
Prayer, coming as it does from Paternoster. This pun makes the
line the cleverest in the poem, and is a stroke of wit of a sort not
often seen in Owen.

The fifth line returns to the question of funeral rites for the
dead soldiers and Owen dismisses the 'mockery' of a conventional religious ceremony. As in 'Greater Love', he feels that
the soldiers' offering has been too much to be made good by
mere hollow formalities:

> No mockeries now for them; no prayers nor bells,
> Nor any voice of mourning save the choirs,—
> The shrill, demented choirs of wailing shells;

Again, as with the prayers, the weapons must provide the only
appropriate cry—even the purest ceremony would be a sacrilege.
The choir must be the shells; their wailing is sufficient, and like
the men it is the mad wailing for the dead in what is an insane
situation.

With the final line of the octave Owen prepares for the
transition to the much quieter sestet where he begins to supply a
picture of the type of remembrance that might just be com-
mensurate with the men's offering. The clamour is taken from
the poem at the line:

> And bugles calling for them from sad shires.

The pace slows, reduced by the effect on the reader of 'calling
for them from', which needs careful enunciation, and the 'sad
shires' with its soft alliteration prepares us for the sestet. The
'sad shires' has a double meaning. The shires may be their
various counties, and the bugles may be an allusion to cow horns
and the rustic origins of most of the ordinary soldiers. This is an

example of possible influence by Housman. The 'sad shires', however, is more likely in this context to refer to the various regiments,
normally spoken of as the ——shire Infantry, the ——shire
Artillery, etc. The bugles sound a recall, but of course there is no
one to return. This calling by bugle, once used to call cows for
milking, also takes us back to the first line of the poem, and so as
well as having a quietening, slowing effect on the pace of the
verse, it also has a structural significance in the poem.

The sestet, however, is not as inventive or as interesting. The
conventional emblems of mourning are considered—candles,
palls and flowers—and again all dismissed as mere trappings.
The nearest to true mourning, claims Owen, will be the cherished
memories of the soldiers:

> Not in the hands of boys, but in their eyes
> Shall shine the holy glimmers of good-byes.
> The pallor of girls' brows shall be their pall;
> Their flowers the tenderness of patient minds,

The poem ends with the symbolic image of the drawing of blinds,
an image associated with mourning and also reminiscent of the
phrase 'in the evening and at the ending of the day, we will
remember them'. The alliterated d's of the last line again give
the poem a feeling of finality, even though the action is one that
will be repeated indefinitely.

What appears unsatisfactory in the sestet, however, is some of
Owen's diction, which is too Victorian, too Pre-Raphaelite. 'The
pallor of girls' brows', for instance, is rather precious, as is the
expression 'the tenderness of patient minds'. The image of 'holy
glimmers' shining in boys' eyes is all very well for the front of a
too-sickly Christmas card, but how many eyes really show a holy
glow of remembrance? Thus, while we can understand Owen's
feeling that only in genuine sadness and remembrance can the
soldiers' sacrifice be truly celebrated, we are rather at odds to
accept the languid images he presents us with as examples of the
sort of mourning he thinks appropriate.

So, like many of Owen's poems, this is a work of uneven
quality. In its expression of the idea of the unappreciated and
unsullied sacrifice of the soldiers, however, it exceeds 'Greater
Love' in concise effectiveness.

The Send-Off

This poem attacks the indifference of a nation that could send thousands of men to fight and die and yet had little real concern for them. It is filled with images of conspiracy and hypocrisy.

As the soldiers march off from their training camp at the beginning of the poem, there is straightaway a sinister element at work:

> Down the close, darkening lanes they sang their way
> To the siding-shed,

The lane is 'close' to begin with, but then it is 'darkening'. The use of this participle suggests the darkness of the plot closing in around the ingenuous soldiers who sing quite happily as if nothing was happening to them. The length of the first line seems to protract the feeling of encircling darkness, till the abrupt second line brings us back to earth. Owen is explaining the soldiers' unconcern by contrasting the sinister nature of the plot with the very subtle and seemingly everyday setting of it. Yet it might be noticed that they are shipped off from a siding-shed, rather like cattle being led off to slaughter. The siding-shed is off the main track and so a further note of guilty covering-up is added. On the train, however, as they line the windows to say good-bye to the women, there is a suggestion given by 'grimly gay' that they are uneasy and suspicious. Owen does not justify this feeling, though, until two lines later. The soldiers have stuck sprays of flowers, given to them by their wives and girlfriends, into their tunic breasts and Owen sees this white like the flowers on a dead man's chest—or perhaps with 'spray' he is thinking of froth or foam on a dead man. The introduction of the word 'dead' has a shattering effect, and Owen deliberately places it at the end of a line and a sentence to force the reader to pause and consider its implications:

> Their breasts were stuck all white with wreath and spray
> As men's are, dead.

But this impact is soon annulled by the indifference of those around:

> Dull porters watched them, and a casual tramp
> Stood staring hard,
> Sorry to miss them from the upland camp.

The words 'dull' and 'casual' convey the total apathy that all around feel for these men who are already being written off by Owen as 'dead', so sure is their fate. The most the tramp will do is to 'stare'; he will miss them, but we are left with the impression that he will soon be able to find some new pastime. The intrigue really begins with:

> Then, unmoved, signals nodded, and a lamp
> Winked to the guard.

and the men are off to their deaths as simply as that. The images of nodding and winking refer to conventional parts of any plot, but notice Owen strikes a little paradox when he says, 'Then, unmoved'. The 'unmoved' expresses another angle of the feeling-lessness of the plan and, because a signal must actually move to be noticed, the idea is more striking. It is an emotional un-involvement which refers to the men and women watching as it appears to do to the signal.

No sooner has Owen despatched the soldiers, though, mention-ing the sense of guilt which is in the onlookers

> So secretly, like wrongs hushed-up, they went.

than he demonstrates the vehemence with which all concerned deny any knowledge or part in the operation:

> They were not ours:
> We never heard to which front these were sent.

As in lines 1 and 2, the long line 11 serves as a slow build up to lines 12 and 13 with their frantic denials, made still more biting by our awareness that the soldiers were fighting for the very people who, with 'They were not ours', imply that they do not even accept them as being part of the nation.

Again in lines 14 and 15, no concern is felt for whether the soldiers are alive or dead:

> Nor there if they yet mock what women meant
> Who gave them flowers.

If the flowers given to them as signs of devotion are now serving as wreaths on their corpses, this will not affect the short memories of those alive at home.

The final stanza takes the hope that victory offers and shows that even if they do 'win' this war (and after so much death and destruction, Owen is quite sure no nation can possibly be thought victorious), the triumphant return promised will be a hollow sham.

> Shall they return to beatings of great bells
> In wild train loads?

The soldiers may go off in 'grimly gay' train loads, but they will return differently:

> A few, a few, too few for drums and yells,
> May creep back, silent, to still village wells
> Up half-known roads.

The repetition of 'few' stresses the enormous difference in numbers who return to those who go away. They may 'creep' back, as opposed to how they marched off in the beginning. They will be silent now, compared with their singing as they left. And though the lanes were sinister with the darkness of conspiracy when they left, now they are only 'half-known' for the men's minds have been destroyed by war.

This is a most moving and convincing poem. It illustrates once more Owen's feeling that people at home are apathetic towards the fate of the soldiers, concerned only with how the men's leaving will affect them. The poem is well constructed and the language suited to the subject. We may feel that Owen is excessively bitter, but he had to rouse his readers into consciousness of what was happening. He was, after all, a mouthpiece for his fellow soldiers.

Exposure

As Owen repeats at the end of four of the stanzas, 'nothing happens' in this poem. It is a poem, though, where many of the thoughts of the men are set out and explored, and it is not localized but applies to soldiers everywhere on every side, for all of them, at heart, have the same basic feelings, doubts and dreams. At the end we are left asking the question; if nothing happens why is everyone continuing with this appalling procedure, why don't they all just stop? There is no answer, of course.

The poem begins with a reference to the intense cold, and the violent metaphor 'knive us' is used to convey the vicious nature of the cold that freezes to the brain, dulling the senses and inhibiting thought. Throughout, the weather is presented as being a more terrible enemy than the opposing army—and, of course, it is an enemy which affects both armies, thus displaying the universal nature of the poem. Having adjusted to the continual noise of battle, the men are kept awake by the silence. Even quietness brings with it fear:

> Worried by silence, sentries whisper, curious, nervous,
> But nothing happens.

The flares, instead of permitting them to see if all is well, only confuse the men. The 'salient' is a name for part of the military fortifications and their memory of what this is like is obscured by the distorting light. Salient also means that which is important, and so Owen uses it in a double sense by claiming that the continued state of anxiety and cold disrupts their previously held values.

Stanza two brings a note of unreality into the poem. The barbed wire is likened to a bramble bush and the wind seems to be caught in it. In the north the guns flash and the sound is so distant that it seems to be 'some other war'. Owen asks the same question as the reader feels inclined to ask at the end:

> What are we doing here?

During reports of fighting and direct attack, the soldiers' situation is justified—no matter how unjustified the war itself may be— but at moments of inactivity with only the elements as enemy the question (which could be asked by the enemy's troops also) is a particularly distressing one.

The cold dawn brings new miseries and it is spoken of as if it were an enemy amassing its troops for a fresh assault:

> Dawn massing in the east her melancholy army
> Attacks once more in ranks on shivering ranks of gray,
> But nothing happens.

The soldiers are so stunned that reality has left them; they know only their current situation:

> We only know war lasts, rain soaks, and clouds sag
> > stormy.

Stanza four opens with a burst of action, as some enemy bullets are fired past them, but the men have a more frightening enemy to contend with, the weather which is, compared with bullets:

> Less deathly than the air that shudders black with
> > snow,

The snow appears to fall carelessly at first, but then it becomes more sinister, likened to a strangler that feels for the men's faces.

> Pale flakes with fingering stealth come feeling for our
> > faces—

The silentness and yet the deadliness of snow is brought out in this image. The men retreat in fear, they 'cringe' in holes for protection and there they dream of their homes and pleasant times before the war began:

> . . . So we drowse, sun-dozed,
> Littered with blossoms trickling where the
> > blackbird fusses.

Here Owen introduces a recurring theme, that if they are happy they must be dead or dying, since living is so bad:

> Is it that we are dying?

Still in this dream state, the men imagine they are returning to their homes, but they find them shut up; the fires are low and the house is occupied only by the mice:

> Shutters and doors, all closed: on us the doors
> > are closed,—
> We turn back to our dying.

so they return to their trenches where they will die.

The next stanza reflects a lack of faith on the part of many of the soldiers. Will the fires of love ever burn again? Will the sun shine on children or fields or fruit? Will the spring ever come? The men fear it may not. They have always believed in these things before as inevitabilities, 'Since we believe not otherwise', but now, 'For God's invincible spring our love is made afraid'. Since they doubt even the purpose of life, they die more willingly:

> For love of God seems dying.

Faith has become harder to accept in view of what they have and can see around them. In a formless world is there any point in living? Clearly, many soldiers do not believe that there is.

The last stanza returns to the theme of the cold, and takes us full-circle back to the beginning. The intense frost, which is 'His', God's frost, further stresses the seeming purposelessness in life. The frost will kill and maim; how can it come from a loving creator-God. And yet *it* is there. The question it begs is, is the loving God there? Owen gives no answer, but significantly describes a burying party whose hands can barely hold their picks and shovels. They make their way through the dead men unable to fully recognize any and—nothing happens.

Though nothing may appear to happen, because no action is being fought, much in fact does occur. Men lose their faith, they recall past situations, they wish for death. The line 'But nothing happens' assumes ironic qualities when we realize that during this lull in the fighting a great deal is happening, but it is happening within the men themselves, which is after all equally important as what is happening in the fighting.

This poem is notable for Owen's use of half-rhyme. In stanza one, for example, 'knive us' is set against 'nervous'; 'silent' against 'salient', and the final half-line stands out prominently because it neither rhymes nor in any way approaches para-rhyme. Similarly, in stanza two, 'wire' and 'war', 'brambles' and 'grumbles' are offset, and so on throughout the poem. The effect of this rather ugly form of word-play is to stress the ugliness of the situation.

The Show

This is not a difficult poem to understand. It is based on the simple idea that Owen imagines himself detached from the battlefield, giving him an objective view of a situation. The scene is depicted as if from above where the physical landscape is described in terms of desolation and disease. From this distanced position even the division between armies is insignificant—they appear merely as two different-coloured lines. At the end of the poem, though, the two lines engage in fighting and Owen falls and is shown by a personification of death the dead men, among whom he finds himself. That, then, is what the poem is about. It has one or two interesting features, however, not least among which is his diversity of description of the scene. The versification is interesting too, as the poem is not broken up into stanzas but into separate sentences, some of three and four lines coming between the more frequent couplets and adding variety to the poem.

The poem opens somewhat mysteriously with Owen's soul in the company of Death and above the battle area. No explanation is given as to how he comes to be there, 'As unremembering how I rose or why', and from then on he describes what he sees below. The earth is described as a rotting, maggot-infested corpse with the soldiers as the maggots crawling about its corruption. The land is 'sad', 'weak' and 'sweats'. Images of disease are piled up: 'pocks', 'scabs of plagues' and 'warts' are all used to indicate the state of pollution. Not surprisingly, the earth smells appropriately decayed.

> (And smell came up from those foul openings
> As out of mouths, or deep wounds deepening.)

The place is a 'mire' over which 'moved thin caterpillars' which seem to 'writhe' and 'shrivel' along 'slimy paths'.

> From gloom's last dregs these long-strung creatures
> crept,
> And vanished out of dawn down hidden holes.

Eventually, as the description becomes more vivid, we realize
that his long strings like caterpillars, some brown, some gray,
are, in fact, the two lines of opposing soldiers—the British in
brown, the Germans in gray. The spines he talks of are the
barrels of the guns protruding from the trenches which are the
'ditches' and 'slimy paths' that had been 'trailed and scraped'.
Both sides are seen impartially, they are

> All migrants from green fields, intent on mire.

It is not until there is a surge forward in the gray line, however,
that Owen falls from his omniscient position. It appears from his
height that one 'caterpillar' launches—he uses 'ramped' meaning
stormed—itself upon the other and begins to eat it. He sees the
contortions as the two lines struggle:

> I saw their bitten backs curve, loop, and straighten,
> I watched those agonies curl, lift, and flatten.

and it is at this point that he falls to earth. This fall, however,
does not bring him back to actual reality, for Death falls with
him and shows him the feet of a man half hidden in the earth.
They could be the feet of any man, until he realizes, on being
shown his own severed head, that they are his.

   This poem is formless like the nightmare that it is. It is not
particularly imaginative and the descriptions are not out-
standingly original, but it has its strengths, of which Owen's
unbiased viewpoint is one. Technically, there are many good
examples of half-rhyme used to effect: 'hills' and 'holes', 'more'
and 'mire', 'mean' and 'moan', 'hid' and 'head', all of which
emphasize by their disagreeable dissonance the foulness of the
subject.

Spring Offensive

Here Owen considers the effects of tension and fighting on the
soldiers, as he does in 'Insensibility'. The poem refers to no
specific encounter but, again, has a universal application.

   It begins in a tranquil atmosphere. There is almost the feeling
that we are joining a picnic party:

> Halted against the shade of a last hill,
> They fed, and lying easy, were at ease
> And, finding comfortable chests and knees,
> Carelessly slept.

But the phrase 'a last hill' is somehow rather disconcerting: it
offers us no positive information but leaves us with the question,
how the *last* hill? The stress of 'easy' and 'ease' is somehow just
too conspicuous; and that they 'carelessly' slept makes us conscious that perhaps their inattention is a form of negligence.
Certainly, the tranquillity dissolves in the second part of the
stanza with the lines

> . . . But many there stood still
> To face the stark, blank sky beyond the ridge,
> Knowing their feet had come to the end of the world.

Now we realize that the troops are at the front line. We also
notice a distinction between those who can sleep and the 'many'
who are too nervous to do so. This is redolent of the 'lucky'
insensible men who were by then immune to fear having adjusted
to live with it.

The second stanza deals with the thoughts of these men who
watch the beauties of nature in spring and, though partially
released from their fears by them, are nonetheless always conscious of what is just ahead over the line of grass:

> For though the summer oozed into their veins
> Like an injected drug for their bodies' pains,
> Sharp on their souls hung the imminent line of grass,

Right from the beginning of the poem Owen is building up
tension and he does this in the third stanza by tacitly contrasting
the beauty of nature with the ugliness of the impending fighting.
The scene seems to be almost too serene: the 'warm field', the
buttercups, the bramble bushes, and all stretching into 'the far
valley behind'. Only two slight discords upset the peace of this
description, the 'slow' of the soldiers' boots and the 'sorrowing
hands' of the bushes. The buttercups have covered the soldiers'
boots in pollen but the footsteps themselves have been reluctant
ones:

> Had blessed with gold their *slow* boots coming up,

As they walk past, the 'little' brambles try to hold them back, to prevent them going to their deaths:

> . . . even the little brambles would not yield,
> But clutched and clung to them like sorrowing hands;

In stanza four the tension is again increased, more obviously this time, as they are given the signal to make ready. There is no commotion, no calling out.

> Only a lift and flare of eyes. . . .

The soldiers stop looking at the sun and prepare for the engagement. In stanza five they reach the top of the hill and as they go over, so the poem reaches its peak of tension. Note how the rapid action is brought to a sudden halt on 'Exposed':

> So, soon they topped the hill, and raced together
> Over an open stretch of herb and heather
> Exposed. . . .

But after this pause with its suspense, the effect of the attack is made to seem doubly violent:

> Exposed. And instantly the whole sky burned
> With fury against them; . . .

The buttercups become cups to catch the soldiers' blood and the green slope that had so captivated the men is now

> Chasmed and steepened sheer to infinite space.

It is almost as if the hill had two sides of which one is peaceful and lovely and the other an unknown inferno.

After the break in the poem, Owen is more concerned with examining the effects on the survivors. Those who are dead are no more, they have gone 'past this world's verge'. There is a hesitancy, however, about what Owen thinks may have happened to them in death.

> *Some say* God caught them even before they fell.

The comforting belief in their divine aid is severed by the sceptical phrase 'some say'. But Owen, as he says in his Preface, was not writing poems of consolation.

The final stanza deals with the men who survive the attack. Not surprisingly, they do not wish to talk of those who 'went under'. What, Owen asks, of the men who went into this hell and, by actions 'out-fiending all its fiends and flames', made it back to life? It is noteworthy that he does not attribute their escape to any traditional sense of valour, but to 'superhuman inhumanities', 'immemorial shames'. Yet, having got back to this side, they do not talk of what has taken place. Owen leaves us to consider why, but has, of course, subtly given us the answer in his listing of the 'superhuman inhumanities'. These men are conscious of having acted bestially in order to survive; they know that their violence saved their lives, but they know too that morally their actions were odious, and so they sit silent.

This is a very fine poem, calculated in its tension and effect, and never once do we feel that Owen is not certain of what he is conveying. The contrasts between the men who can sleep, insensible of fear, and those who are still nervous; between the beauty of nature one moment and its ugliness the next; between the beauty of nature and the vileness of the soldiers' actions; between the optimism of some and his own scepticism and between the dead and the survivors, all keep it vitally alive. The penetration which Owen displays as he looks into the men before the encounters and the men who survive it is remarkably incisive. The language of the poem is unselfconscious; there are no unnecessary or ornate words; nothing is archaic or quaint. Instead we have a functioning language used to create effects as varied as tranquillity and the utmost tension within a few lines. Altogether, it is a very finely wrought and highly moving poem.

Dulce Et Decorum Est

As we have seen, the many patriotic poems produced by people who knew nothing of the soldiers' war incensed Owen. On the appearance of a particularly hollow one by a woman called Jessie Pope, he determined to refute once and for all 'the old lies' that it contained—consequently he wrote 'Dulce Et Decorum Est'. In his original draft he addressed it 'To a certain Poetess' in an effort to outface all such authors. This is possibly Owen's best known poem. Its nightmarish combination of realistic reporting and silencing rhetoric caught the public imagination as few of his other poems have. But popularity and critical approbation are often removed and here Owen's main flaw, apart from a few rather sound-governed phrases, is that he reaches the same undisciplined heights, almost ranting, as did 'the certain Poetess' herself.

The poem falls into four sections: a description of the men's numbed, shell-shocked condition; an account of a gas-attack; its haunting effect on Owen; and finally, after these descriptions, a passage of invective culminating in the rousing climax of the last two lines. Down to the last section it is very fine. It is when he is being dismissive that he loses control slightly, as will be seen.

The poem begins with a description of the men as they trudge through mud from the front line back to their base camp for rest. At the beginning, however, we would not know that Owen was talking about fighting men at all:

> Bent double, like old beggars under sacks,
> Knock-kneed, coughing like hags, we cursed through
> sludge,

The image of the exhausted soldiers, like ragged beggars, is the exact opposite to that which the British Expeditionary Force must have conjured up in the British people's minds. Even heading for rest they cannot hurry. Owen uses 'cursed' as if it were a verb describing their walk, and trudging evokes all the lassitude of the journey to their 'distant' rest. The men without boots limp on, but not bare-foot—their feet are covered in blood! Incoherent with tiredness, their senses have almost gone!

> Men marched asleep. Many had lost their boots
> But limped on, blood-shod. All went lame; all blind;
> Drunk with fatigue; deaf even to the hoots
> Of tired, outstripped Five-Nines that dropped behind.

The short phrases, each with the long pause which the sense and the semi-colon dictates, list in a quite simple way the soldiers' troubles. Even the imminent danger of the dropping shells does not hurry or frighten them. The shells, too, are 'tired', and they are 'outstripped', surpassed in deadliness by the men's fatigue. So Owen presents the picture of weary men fighting a weary war to contradict the image of the indefatigable 'British Soldier' of the jingoistic rhymes.

Suddenly the poem springs into action at the word 'Gas'. Notice the rhythm of the line:

> Gas! Gas! Quick, boys!—An ecstasy of fumbling,

The 'Gas' cry comes in two monosyllabic stabs and 'Quick, boys!' is equally acute, but then the dash introduces a pause before we return to watch these exhausted soldiers fumbling for gas-masks. In their dazed condition they cannot slip the helmets on quickly, but because they are fumbling for their lives there is a wildness, an 'ecstasy' about it. Owen appears to be using 'ecstasy' here in its older sense meaning madness.[1] They cannot be groping for gas-masks in pleasure, as the modern meaning would suggest, and we know that Owen is fond of the old-fashioned use of words. But not everyone fits his mask in time and one soldier is poisoned by the gas.

> But someone still was yelling out and stumbling
> And flound'ring like a man in fire or lime . . .

The gas was mustard-gas or phosgene which would burn its victim just as fire or lime might do. Owen, however, goes a step further in this lurid description by using words normally associated with death by drowning: 'flound'ring', 'plunges', and 'drowning' itself. The reason for these images is that when men inhaled the poisonous gas it attacked the tissues of the lung, and they literally drowned in their own blood and the lining of their lungs was rotted in a few seconds. So the image of drowning is not only appropriate because the man's tired, dying actions would be like a swimmer, not only because the gas is green like the sea, but also because he was in a real sense 'drowning'.

> Dim, through the misty panes and thick green light,
> As under a green sea, I saw him drowning.

[1] See references to ecstasy in this sense in *Macbeth* and *Hamlet*.

The next two lines form the third section of the poem in which Owen mentions that he is haunted by nightmares of this event. Already, of course, there have been nightmarish qualities displayed in the poem: the man's slow-motion struggles, the 'haunting' flares which cast an eerie white light over the land, and the haglike appearance of the soldiers. Now, in his dreams, Owen sees the man suffering still:

> In all my dreams, before my helpless sight,
> He plunges at me, guttering, choking, drowning.

'Guttering' suggests the extinguishing of the small flame of life that was still in the man. 'Choking' and 'drowning' we know apply both literally and metaphorically. And Owen's sense of guilt at his own inadequacy to help is perhaps the strongest sensation which haunts him—'before my *helpless* sight'. The guilt is emphasized because the dying man 'plunges at' him, almost accusingly as if demanding aid and desperately attacking him to gain it.

Having built up a picture, then, of the men's condition in general and having shown us a gas attack in particular and its effect on him personally, Owen now turns to the patriotic poets. His very first line contains an accusation, though one which is suggested rather than made openly:

> If in some smothering dreams you too could pace

The use of 'smothering dreams' suggests that the nearest these people in Britain will come to the sensations he has just described is if they should dream of it while comfortable in their well-feathered beds. They will 'smother' in comfort not in gas. If they could see the full extent of the horrors of the war, watch 'the white eyes writhing in his face', hear 'at every jolt, the blood/ Come gargling from the froth-corrupted lungs', see the 'vile, incurable sores on innocent tongues', then they would not spread their high-sounding clichés so widely:

> My friend, you would not tell with such high zest
> To children ardent for some desperate glory,
> The old Lie: Dulce et decorum est
> Pro patria mori.

This is a fine rousing end to a poem of signal impact, a poem in which Owen, without ever expressing any self-pity for his own condition, creates such a vivid picture of the general suffering of all the men involved in the war. And yet there is an unmistakable feeling that he falls into the trap of rhetoric himself. In the final section he is building up the intensity of his verse with the various horrific aspects of real life in the trenches, but he uses some meaningless phrases and so, for the intelligent reader, diminishes the effect. 'Like a devil's sick of sin', is an example—how can a devil grow sick of what he is the embodiment of? How can a man's face be compared to a face of an imaginary creature visualized differently by every reader? Similarly, few readers can feel that 'bitter as the cud' has any significant meaning for them. It is not enough to say that they create a certain sensation; poetry is an intellectually as well as an emotionally appealing art and what appeals to our emotions, after all, is what we understand.

This criticism, however, though it dims the poem slightly, should not overshadow a great work of vivid, sensitive description. Although it verges on ranting at the end, it is without bitterness. Notice the use of 'My friend' in line 25, and the sympathetic tolerance conveyed by describing the young soldiers anxious to win glory in war as 'ardent children'. Owen has great sympathy for the suffering men, the misguided 'children', and even for the jingoists. As we know, he is never self-pitying, but concerned and pleading for others.

Asleep

This is a simple poem in which Owen returns to the theme that death is preferable to the hideous life the soldiers lead. In the first section a soldier, described only as exhausted and laden, gently falls asleep and in that sleep is shot. But death, like sleep, is a welcome release from life in the trenches. In the second section, Owen postulates three states, two of which may apply to the soldier and the third to him. The two states for the dead soldier are either heaven or total deadness with no after-life. These are uncertain, but also unimportant—he has his release. The certainty is for those left alive. They must face life, there is no release for them.

The poem begins by showing us the soldier as he lies down to snatch a moment's sleep. Like all the men, he sleeps fully clothed and beside his pack, prepared for an immediate alert. Life is work and no sleep.

> Under his helmet, up against his pack,
> After the many days of work and waking,

Sleep, when it comes, is gentle:

> Sleep took him by the brow and laid him back.

Notice the words which imply this, 'took him by the brow' and 'laid him back'. These are protective actions and death is the same:

> And in the happy no-time of his sleeping,
> Death took him by the heart. . . .

Owen restates the theme that the only happiness for the soldiers is when they are asleep or dead. This one does not struggle to cling to life. It is as if his unconscious mind wills him to die. But we are not yet actually told that he has been shot.

> . . . There was a quaking
> Of the aborted life within him leaping . . .
> Then chest and sleepy arms once more fell slack.

The words 'quaking' and 'leaping' both suggest that he was excited by the chance to relinquish life. After the one move he falls back into what could be a sleep again, a relaxed state conveyed by 'sleepy arms' and 'slack'. It is only at this point that Owen tells us he has been shot—but because it partially disrupts the feeling of the soldier's having wished death to come, the blood is described in terms which show how out of place it is:

> And soon the slow, stray blood came creeping
> From the intrusive lead, like ants on track.

'Stray', 'creeping' and 'intrusive' all convey this. The bullet, we sense, was only coincidental in this soldier's death, it has not shattered or torn as it might have someone who wanted desperately to live. It seems only to have interrupted his dream for a second.

To present a young man with so little will to live is a distressing notion, and Owen is conscious that this can be used to emphasize the hellishness of the soldiers' situation. If the uncertainty of death —and he deals with this uncertainty in the next section—is preferable to life, then life must really be appalling.

In the second section, Owen outlines alternatives for the dead man. Either he may have gone to heaven or he may simply be part of the earth again. Owen's picture of heaven is unrealistic in its childish simplicity, but this is quite deliberate. Heaven is a place of 'great wings', 'High pillowed on calm pillows of God's making', 'Above these clouds'. It is a fairy-tale paradise, and we are left in no doubt as to Owen's belief in its unlikelihood by the way in which he begins with the questioning word 'Whether' and then breaks off and into the more obvious reality with

> —Or whether yet his thin and sodden head
> Confuses more and more with the low mould,

The description of the more likely alternative is not an attractive one. Whether he is part of the 'low mould', 'His hair being one with the grey grass' and his being merely part of the field, what, Owen asks, does it matter, for again he is away from the more horrific reality of life. So if he is in a sugar-candy heaven, he is well off. If he is part of the cold earth, he is equally lucky. The dying of a soldier is commonplace, however, so Owen partially dismisses him.

> Who knows? Who hopes? Who troubles? Let it pass!
> He sleeps. . . .

His fate is certain, he is out of things, but their lives go on and Owen must revert to them again. All that can finally be said is:

> . . . He sleeps less tremulous, less cold
> Than we who must awake, and waking, say Alas!

Waking from the 'no-time' of sleep brings no joy at still being alive but a cry of regret and despair. The war distorts and what is natural in everyday life is unnatural now. There is no regret expressed for the dead soldier, only envy at his release.

This is a moving poem, not because we feel sad at the soldier's death, but because we feel distressed that the other men must live on. By using simple diction and imagery, by keeping the pace measured and even, and by the apparently logical—from his point of view—method of presentation, Owen creates the right degree of emotional involvement in his readers. Again, he expresses a plea for all the men of the war. He speaks of 'we', not 'I'. He does not make any special case for himself as a poet or an especially sensitive being, but draws our attention to their common plight who 'waking say Alas!'

Futility

Although as a young man Owen was quite strongly religious, and from 1911 till 1913 was pupil and lay assistant to the vicar of Dunsden in Oxfordshire, his experiences in the war considerably altered his religious beliefs. His logic is easily understandable: 'How could a God who is loving and all-powerful allow this to happen?' Finding no answer to this question, he questioned his earlier belief in God, and since he saw the teaching of the church as quite contrary to Christ's *real* message, he rejected the church completely.

> Already I have comprehended a light which will never filter into the dogma of any national church: namely that one of Christ's essential commands was, Passivity at any price! Suffer dishonour and disgrace, but never resort to arms.
> (From a letter to his mother, 2 May 1917)

Although 'Futility' is not actively anti-religious, Owen implies his disbelief in God by ignoring the possibility of His existence and ascribing the power of life and creation to the sun. The 'futility' might be seen to be three-fold: (a) the futility of the young man having given his life in the war for nothing, (b) the futility of hoping in religion and the power of God to change the situation, and (c) the futility of trying to see a logic behind the creation of the world: 'Was it for this the clay grew tall?'

The poem moves at a very gentle pace, in keeping with the tenderness that Owen feels for this young man who has come from his farm to die in the trenches:

> Move him into the sun—
> Gently its touch awoke him once,
> At home, whispering of fields unsown.

This atmosphere is created not only by the use of a slow verse-structure, but also by the choice of words. The touch of the early morning sun was 'gentle', it 'whispered' its message to him. There is no urgency implied and the notion of his previously unhurried life under a gentle—almost paternal—sun is advanced by the words which suggest continuous actions:

> . . . *whispering* of fields unsown.
> *Always* it woke him, even in France,

Though the easy pace is maintained, at line 5 the idea of the continuous nature of the sun's protective influence is broken with the introduction of 'Until':

> Until this morning and this snow.

The stressing of 'this' again halts the feeling that his life was continuous, and counteracts the use of 'Always' by bringing us to one specific time. Clearly, the soldier has died in the cold, but it is also significant that when the sun is hidden, this young man who has led a simple life farming under its protection should die. The last two lines of the stanza declare that the sun is their only hope, and, of course, by doing so they imply that there is no God to appeal to:

> If anything might rouse him now
> The kind old sun will know.

The fatherly qualities usually associated with God are transferred to the much more pagan sun. As Owen points out, however, it is as a last resort ('If anything . . .'), since the idea of a divine being has been so destroyed for these men by the war, that he does not allow it to enter the poem, even to refute it.

The second stanza deals with the sun as the force which brings spring, and which originally brought about life on earth. Again, Owen does not mention a creator-God, but simply states, as if it is so obvious that no one would question, that the sun is the source of all life on earth:

> Think how it wakes the seeds,—
> Woke, once, the clays of a cold star.

Having established the power of the sun to bring life to 'the clays of a cold star', Owen asks what is so special about this young man that it cannot give him life again:

> Are limbs, so dear-achieved, are sides,
> Full-nerved—still warm—too hard to stir?
> Was it for this the clay grew tall?

The futility of moving him into the sun is brought home to us, but no sooner is it clear than Owen becomes almost aggressive towards the force of creation. 'Was it for this the clay grew tall?' he asks, implying that if this young man's fruitless sacrifice of his life is all that he was born and watched over by the sun for years for, then is not creation itself futile?

> —O what made fatuous sunbeams toil
> To break earth's sleep at all?

At the end of the poem the glory of the sun's creation is dimmed —the sunbeams 'toiled' fatuously to 'break' earth's sleep in the initial act of creation. There is no gentleness in the actions here. 'Break' has obvious overtones of roughness, and Owen uses it to show that if this is all that man was made for, then the wakening of earth was a cruel one—better no life at all.

This is one of Owen's most effective quieter poems. There is no mention of the war, and only one reference to their being in France. There is no ranting against those who caused or are continuing the war here, and no mention of bloodshed (the young man's body is not shattered, it is intact and still warm), but the quiet sorrow and the very much muted anger that Owen presents at the senseless death of this man is more telling in its way than lurid descriptions of the horrors of trench warfare.

The Last Laugh

The last laugh in this poem goes neither to the British nor the German forces, but to what Owen sees as the real enemy, the weapons themselves. He gives each one a character suited to its

qualities or appearance and then tries to illustrate their callousness by having them laugh at the men who are being killed. The
presentation of the weapons as an army of supremely confident,
all-powerful, but jovially deadly enemies contrasted to the much
simpler soldiers is very effective. The fact that the shells and
bayonets are enjoying the war thoroughly is the disconcerting
notion that stresses Owen's theme, that in the war there can be
no human victors.

The directness of the first line is calculated to arrest the reader's
attention:

'O Jesus Christ! I'm hit,' he said; and died.

The natural stresses of the line emphasize 'I'm hit', and the
abrupt 'and died' has a finality, with a full-stop causing us to
pause there. It also marks the end of the soldier's life, and this is
all that he says in the stanza. The amount of human expression
in each stanza is outweighed by the weapons' unfeeling reactions,
which take up four of the five lines of each. The simplicity of the
human statement is also contrasted with the more varied series
of reactions from the weapons. The guns of stanza one are all
personified in almost human scale, so that the smallest, the
Bullets, chirp, the Machine-guns chuckle, and the Big Gun gives
a deep belly-laugh. The soldier is hit and dies instantly, they
laugh and laugh on.

In the second stanza, the simplicity of the soldier dying and
calling on his parents

Another sighed—'O Mother, mother! Dad!'
Then smiled, at nothing, childlike, being dead.

and then smiling in death (with Owen underlining his previously
stated idea, that the men in the trenches smile only in death
because there is no place for smiling in their lives) is compared
with the arrogance and condescension of the weapons:

And the lofty Shrapnel-cloud
Leisurely gestured,—Fool!

The use of 'lofty' and 'leisurely' in describing the Shrapnel-cloud
jars the reader into realization of yet another aspect of the
behaviour of these omnipotent weapons. The dead soldier is
merely a fool, tittered at by the lesser shrapnel splinters.

In the final stanza, a soldier dies thinking of the woman he loves. The callous Bayonets smirk at his last unsophisticated words and his falling to kiss the mud instead of 'My Love'. The weapons are presented at their most appalling now, the Shells are a jeering rabble, the Bayonets are smug and silent and the Gas hisses cynically. The feeling that the laughter goes on indefinitely is well conveyed by leaving the Gas to hiss—an echoing sound emphasized by the alliteration

> And the Gas hissed.

So one is left with the deadly laughter of the Gas—the 'Last Laugh' of the title.

We have come to accept the conventional personification of weapons, and expect guns to rumble alarmingly like thunder, to be deadly and intent on killing; bayonets to be vicious and cold; shells to be searing and explosive. But here Owen presents the weapons with more sophisticated characteristics. What adds to the effect is that he describes their various sounds as laughter. It is, of course, always a mocking laughter with the weapons grinning, guffawing and hissing at the men of both sides who think that *they* are in control.

It ought to be apparent by this point that Owen is using the weapons to associate and draw into the poem some of the larger factors in the war. In a way, they can be seen to symbolize all the impersonal aspects which accompany a war of the scale of World War I. He is stressing the fact that these forces rather than human control keep it going—just as if the guns were actually fighting on their own. By surprising our imaginations, he is able to attack the degree of dehumanization behind the war's continuance—and, of course, by implication he attacks those who are responsible for this state of affairs.

This poem illustrates the futility of the war for *all* the parties involved. The only 'virtue' in it is that at least for the impersonal factors it is amusing; for no matter which side wins, the last laugh goes to them, and all they represent.

The Letter

In this poignant little poem a soldier is writing to his wife just before he is suddenly killed. The letter begins with the address—with the British Expeditionary Force—the date and salutation, and into it Owen sets, in brackets, asides by the soldier to his friend. The platitudes in the letter, giving a favourable picture of the war, contrasted with the reality of the asides emphasize the irony of the situation.

From the first two lines we can tell several things about the writer of the letter, and all of them show us a very ordinary soldier. He is not, judging from his diction, very well educated; he is not of very high social position, writing in pencil and addressing his wife not by name but as 'Dear Wife', but he is a human being and though his sentiments are commonplace, they are sincere. His death mattered as much to Owen as the death of a fellow-officer would have done. The main part of the letter is a touching effort to settle any anxieties his wife may have for his well-being, and so he lists all the reassuring but meaningless phrases he can think of:

> I'm in the pink at present, dear.

and,

> We're out of harm's way, not bad fed.

But the falseness of these statements appears from what he says, not in what he writes. Just after writing he's 'not bad fed', he is asking for a bite of bread from his friend.

> '(Say, Jimmie, spare's a bite of bread.)'

Throughout the poem there is a pathetic optimism on the soldier's part that the war will soon be over

> I think the war will end this year.

and,

> I'll soon be 'ome. You mustn't fret.

The irony of his position really becomes apparent, however, when he is shot and then the letter takes on a more moving complexion. To begin with, though, the poem is almost amusingly mundane. The enemy are 'them square-'eaded 'Uns'; he thinks of the pleasant aspects of home life, 'I'm longing for a taste of your old buns'; he has a mock-quarrel with his friend, 'Yer what? Then don't, yer ruddy cow!/And give me back me cigarette!'; and, typically, even in the midst of a European war, he becomes tongue-tied, 'There don't seem much to say just now'. Altogether, a picture of any ordinary soldier writing—which does not come easy to him—to his wife of the routine details of life in the army, concerned for his stomach, his feet, and his family.

> Kiss Nell and Bert. When me and you—

But here he is interrupted by an order to 'Stand to'. Just before this the poem was punctuated ironically with a crashing shell:

> We're out in rest now. Never fear.
> (VRACH! By crumbs, but that was near.)

The written assurance of his safety is violently at odds with reality, as the crashing shell illustrates.

With the order to 'stand to' the soldier abandons the letter, appropriately just at the point where he is about to express some hopes or plans for his life after the war. There are only a few minutes of life left for him. He is hit and at once realizes he is dying. Notice the effectively broken-up line in which Owen sets out in a staccato manner the rapid events:

> Guh! Christ! I'm hit. Take 'old. Aye, bad.

We can feel from the sound and rhythm of the line, the soldier crumpling up. His 'Aye, bad' is a deliberate understatement by Owen, because the man is fatally wounded and knows it. It stresses the sort of stoical acceptance of these things as part of the soldier's life. To the young man's 'Aye, bad' the only available medical aid is a run-of-the-mill antiseptic which is refused with understandable brusqueness:

> No, damn your iodine.

The grandeur of the 'British Expeditionary Force' is reduced to nothing at the total inadequacy which offering a dying man some iodine implies, and this is bitter and effective comment on Owen's part. Similarly, the hollow phrases of comfort to his wife are put into grim proportion when the reality of the war overtakes this soldier. His final wish is that his friend writes to his wife:

> Write my old girl, Jim, there's a dear.

and we assume that he dies on those words.

The overall impression of this poem is one of intense sympathy. The touching concern for his wife and family and the soldier's jokes with his friend are all set into stark relief against the suddenness of his death. Owen carefully modulates the tone of this poem so that what begins as an amusing and ironic contrast between actual conditions and the diluted account in the letter, suddenly becomes a tragic situation into which the humour of the beginning adds a heightened sense of pathos. It is an instance of Owen raising an obviously uneducated, unsophisticated, common soldier to the level of a thoughtful, kind-hearted human figure and then by having him killed, producing a feeling of loss that we can all relate to quite easily. The effect is a highly plaintive one and, as we know, Owen has only chosen one soldier to illustrated what happened to thousands; during the First World War, as many as 50,000 men might die every day.

In this unaffected poem, he creates a universality and a sympathy which is more affecting than all the lurid descriptions of trench conditions. By choosing a soldier almost at random, he is stressing that each death is an irreplaceable loss. As we have seen, it is this capacity for identification with personal tragedy that is the basis of Owen's appeal.

The Sentry

Here Owen is retelling an actual event that happened when he and his men had captured an enemy shelter during an attack. He returns to the vivid descriptive accuracy of such poems as 'Dulce Et Decorum Est' and 'The Show' to create his effect.

The poem begins by a simple narration to set the scene. They have captured an enemy bunker and the enemy are retaliating with heavy fire. As always, the weather is a greater enemy than the German forces. At least the shelter saves those inside it from the bombing, but the rain and cold cannot be kept out. The conditions are appalling:

> Rain, guttering down in waterfalls of slime,
> Kept slush waist-high and rising hour by hour, . . .
> . . . With fumes of whizz-bangs, and the smell of men
> Who'd lived there years, and left their curse in the den,
> If not their corpses. . . .

It is in this foetid setting, then, that the event which is the centre of the poem occurs.

With an echo of 'Anthem for Doomed Youth', we hear of the men being '*herded* from the blast', but inside they are relatively safe. The sentry, however, is outside and with a particularly accurate hit he is blown down into the dug-out. Owen adds touches, of course, which bring an atmosphere of realism to the poem when he describes not only the sound of the shell, but its impact, 'Buffeting eyes and breath, snuffing the candles'. Anyone could imagine a shell exploding, but only someone who had been there could describe the less obvious effects. The sentry's body falls like a dead weight:

> And thud! flump! thud! down the steep steps came
> thumping
> And sploshing in the flood, deluging muck—
> The sentry's body; . . .

He is blown in, along with a cascade of mud and bomb-handles, and is taken for dead until they 'dredge' him up and he 'whines':

> "O sir, my eyes—I'm blind—I'm blind, I'm blind!"

The repetition of the word 'blind' is, of course, to stress the awful nature of the man's injury and that he knows it himself. Hopelessly, Owen holds a candle to his eyes to find out if he can see any glimmer of light at all, but the sentry can see nothing. Owen's kindness in offering some hope is in vain, but the tenderness of the action is embodied in the word 'coaxing'. The memory of the soldier, 'Eyeballs, huge-bulged like squids', seems to haunt

Owen still. The nightmarish quality of the incident is already apparent in the poem but Owen mentions how, like the gassed man of 'Dulce Et Decorum Est', the sentry's eyes 'Watch my dreams still'.

The realism of the situation is not lost with this personal note, for with typical honesty, Owen reports that a new man had to be posted straightaway and normal conditions maintained:

> . . . . but I forgot him there
> In posting Next for duty, and sending a scout
> To beg a stretcher somewhere, and flound'ring about
> To other posts under the shrieking air.

He is also informing his readers that events of this type, though still appalling, are usual enough to be forgotten about after a few minutes. In the midst of continual devastation one badly wounded man can only be spared a few minutes, and the scout is sent to 'beg' a stretcher after all.

In the final section of the poem we are made aware that this was not the only casualty of that attack.

> Those other wretches, how they bled and spewed,
> And one who would have drowned himself for good,—
> I try not to remember these things now.

but Owen permits himself, with some trepidation, to recall just a postscript to this incident.

> Let dread hark back for one word only . . .
> Through the dense din, I say, we heard him shout
> "I see your lights!" But ours had long died out.

This final frantic effort by the sentry is futile. There are no lights to see, he is imagining them. The poem implies that he is not only blinded but affected mentally too, and the tragedy stems from Owen's total inability to offer him any hope.

This poem makes three different assaults upon its readers. It tells of the fate of one soldier in one dug-out at one time during four years, and automatically suggests that this was the fate of hundreds, if not thousands, of similar men. It outlines the conditions which were generally prevalent in the trenches in an attempt to 'educate' its readers. It illustrates the effect of such

W.O.P.—3*

incidents upon Owen who, though he can adjust and forget them in the unnatural conditions of war, is haunted by them in nightmares.

Owen creates most of his impact by the use of effective diction. Again, there is no 'poetic' diction. He uses slang: 'Boche' for German, 'whizz-bangs' for shells and 'crumps', army slang for exploding shells. He uses words with highly unpleasant connotations to describe their situation most fully: 'guttering' suggests overflowing channels; 'slime' suggests sticky, exuding mud; 'slush' is cold and miserable; 'murk' suggests the thickness of the putrid air that fills the shelter; and 'curse' and 'corpses' conjure images of excrement and rotting flesh. The overall effect is an atmosphere of death and decay. 'Herded' has already been mentioned, but other words effectively describe the men's struggle through 'slush waist-high': 'deluging', 'dredged', 'flound'ring'. The men 'bleed' and 'spew', the shells 'pummel' and 'slog', both of which suggest relentless hammering. Owen also uses a large number of onomatopoeic words: 'whizz-bangs', 'thud! flump!', 'sploshing', all convey meaning through their sound. Alliteration also figures in this poem. In the line

> And gave us h*ell*, for sh*ell* on frantic sh*ell*

the repeated 'l' sounds convey the sense of hammering of the falling shells. And again:

> Of old *B*oche *b*ombs, and mud in *r*uck on *r*uck. . . .
> And said if he could see the *l*east *bl*urred *l*ight.

The detail with which Owen records the atmosphere as well as the events brings this poem to life for the reader—but always there is a reminder that this happened to Owen once, and the implied question, how many times were such conditions borne, and such events passed over when no one was there to record them?

Conscious

From June till November of 1917, Owen was convalescing in Craiglockhart Hospital after being sent home suffering from shell-shock. During those months of slow recovery, in which he was plagued with the nightmares and haunting memories he recalls in so many of his poems, he was able to observe the conditions of many of the soldier patients around him. It was from such observation that 'Conscious' originated. The poem tells, in an impressionistic manner, of a soldier suffering from hysteria and fever and, by showing us how mentally and emotionally destroyed he is, Owen is able to add further weight to his anti-war protestation.

Though the soldier appears to wake at the beginning of the poem, it is only his fingers which wake up. He never comes to total consciousness, as the title ironically indicates:

> His fingers wake and flutter; up the bed.
> His eyes come open with a pull of will,

There is no spontaneity in his actions; his eyes do not flash open, they 'come open', but only after effort. His hand 'flutters' as he nervously takes stock of where he is. He is attracted by the brightly-coloured flowers he can see and diverted by the slow noise of the blind-cord trailing across the window-sill. He has a sort of consciousness, but only enough to take in the bright and noisy surroundings. Here Owen breaks off with significant dots, after which he presents an impressionistic picture of the patient's thoughts? They are disjointed and illogical but they show his mental condition, which is fearful and guilt-ridden:

> What a smooth floor the ward has! What a rug!

These are quite ordinary observations—especially coming from a man used to mud-filled trenches. With the next line, however, comes a note of suspicion:

> Who is that talking somewhere out of sight?

The next line seems to intensify this into fear:

> Why are they laughing? . . .

The final line of the stanza is a hysterical cry:

> "Nurse! Doctor!"—"Yes; all right, all right!"

The calming words, of course, come from the nurse or doctor who has come at his call.

Between stanzas there is a gap while the soldier sleeps, but to him no time seems to have passed, for,

> But sudden evening muddles all the air—

He wakes abruptly and is confused by the passage of time which he has not noticed. Although conscious of sights and sounds, he cannot tackle more difficult reasoning processes.

> There seems no time to want a drink of water,

He cannot understand distance:

> Nurse looks so far away . . .

And all the while the effect of what he has experienced exercises its permanently debilitating force upon him:

> Music and roses burst through crimson slaughter.

The guilt and fear which this has left him with cause everything to be tainted with memories of blood and carnage. It is appropriate that Owen should use the word 'burst', because it has violent associations and this line is one in which the deforming nature of his recent experiences is made most forcefully. Again, in the next line we learn of yet another loss. This time it is his memory.

> He can't remember where he saw blue sky.

This series is broken, however, as the soldier falls into a fever. Though still awake, he is cold and hot by turns, and then his sight fails him:

> And there's no light to see the voices by;

At the very end he again feels the fears and anxieties as before; he wants to ask a question but does not know what it is. It is in this position that Owen leaves us. This he says is a soldier who has escaped with his life. As far as we can tell, he is physically intact, but this only serves as a contrast to his mental incapacitation. Relatively simple reasoning processes are denied him, he is only aware of his immediate physical condition and his all-pervading fear and guilt. The cause of this destruction is made all too obvious in line 12. This, says Owen, is a man who has 'survived'. He has not been blown apart or otherwise wounded, but consider what is left of him; only a frame with none of the higher senses that make life endurable or even possible. This is the 'conscious', this is a man who might have been thought lucky. The obvious comparisons to what would be considered un-fortunate, Owen leaves unsaid.

Owen's attention to details which could only have been observed first-hand is minutely accurate. The structure of the poem creating the sense of sleep between sections is interesting and effective. Perhaps there is just enough of the feeling of personal recollection on Owen's part to make us aware of the sincerity of his plea. It is not a large-scale work, it is a miniature, yet it is no less disturbing than those poems in which the sights and shells of the trenches are conjured up so vividly. This, says Owen, is the alternative to death.

A Terre

This is subtitled 'Being the Philosophy of Many Soldiers' and the title itself means 'to earth', which recalls the funeral service 'dust to dust'. That we all return to dust some time, claims Owen, is the soldier's belief by which he consoles himself for the fact that he lives with imminent death all the time. To contrast with this, we are listening to the monologue of a badly wounded officer throughout the poem.

The first line gives us an invitation to become involved with his sufferings:

> Sit on the bed. I'm blind, and three parts shell.
> Be careful; can't shake hands now; never shall.

This is the soldier's life. Incapacitated, he is confined to hospital where he cannot see or touch another person, 'three parts shell'. He cannot even shake hands—and the permanence of his isolation is confirmed with 'never shall'. This fragile man shattered by the war now merely exists, and Owen uses his terrible crippled state to highlight his desperation for life—even the vegetable existence of being without physical faculties and control. Luckily, this man has not been mentally broken, as his monologue by its eloquence and intellectual awareness demonstrates. His lack of bodily control is further emphasized in the first stanza, where even here he uses the military expression that his arms have 'mutinied' against him. With 'idle brats' we see the childlike inability of his fingers to function for him.

The effort to remember his position as an officer is borne out in the second stanza

> I tried to peg out soldierly,—no use!

but the second half of the line refutes all the hollow manliness in the first part. Against the empty epithet 'soldierly' comes the very direct force of 'no use!'.

> One dies of war like any old disease.

We have already observed Owen likening the war to a disease, a malady which turns the earth into a corpse. Here, the almost stoical acceptance of the fatality of war is the disconcerting factor. It is simply another disease, just another way of uniting one with the earth. The disease-like qualities of death in its maiming sense we can see from the officer in the poem, but for his effect, Owen relies on our realization that war is not like a disease at all. It is a human invention, it can be prevented, it ought never to occur. After this the narrator of the poem scathingly touches on the 'glories' which war has brought him; medals—bandages for his blinded eyes; ribbons—strips of flesh torn from him 'in scarlet shreds'. Realizing that this expression of the triviality of military decorations (and Owen cannot have been oblivious to the unsightly nature of the wounds, which clashes with the idea of medals as 'decorations') is somewhat 'poetic', the narrator draws our attention to it in a sarcastic '(That's for your poetry book.)'. The importance of the phrase is twofold. First, it shows a consciousness that in conventional war poetry such images are ignored, and so he says accusingly, 'show the truth of the situation for once', and secondly, it shows an alertness on the part of the narrator to avoid what is openly sentimental. Even though he is appallingly wounded, he will not allow himself to be melodramatic and so he rounds on his own self-conscious expression quite severely.

In the third stanza, the officer touches on what he used to think he believed:

> A short life and a merry one, my buck!
> We used to say we'd hate to live dead-old,—
> Yet now. . . .

but that was before death was brought home to him. Now, and throughout the rest of the poem, he develops the same theme. He would assume any role, even any form, human or animal, almost vegetable, so long as he could prolong his life. Owen takes this opportunity to aim a blow at the deliberately 'patriotic' figures whose patriotism has never interfered with the comfortable tenor of their lives:

> . . . I'd willingly be puffy, bald,
> And patriotic.

This, it would appear, was the role which the narrator was brought up to play. What could I teach a son? he asks, and can only reply that he would pass on what he had been taught himself.

> Shooting, war, hunting, all the arts of hurting.
> Well, that's what I learnt,—that, and making money.

There is an alarming pessimism in these lines. Even though this man may have been educated to follow the pattern that led him to his pathetic half-life situation, he seems to have learnt no more from his experience in the war. He is unable to break away from the ideas of aggression and self-advancement he learnt and to teach his son, if he had one, a different set of values reflecting his mature experience. In the circumstances, this is a rather despairing revelation. Owen does not dwell on it, however, but passes on to a more sympathetic vein. It is characteristic that he shades in this gloomy aspect of the man's personality but does not score it deeply. His capacity for understanding overcomes again and the clash between the last words of stanza three and the ideas expressed in stanza four is vivid.

> . . . God! For one year
> To help myself to nothing more than air!

His 'money making' upbringing is invalidated by his wish now

for something he cannot possibly buy. Similarly, Owen intends
that as this point is destroyed, so the other aspects of his cramping
previous life will also seem hollow. The plea for life, however, is
a touching one:

> One Spring! Is one too good to spare, too long?
> Spring wind would work its own way to my lung,
> And grow my legs as quick as lilac-shoots.

The officer's faith in the healing power of nature does not take
into account the complete disruption which the war has caused.
Unnatural events have separated man from the natural forces,
so his wish for one more spring is unheeded. Realizing this, the
narrator wishes he could change places with someone who is fit
—the first to spring to mind is his servant who, though lamed, is
still largely unharmed. When life itself is threatened, social
barriers and conventions appear as unimportant in perspective.
The servant is alive, the master is a 'mummy', encased in
bandages. For life he would become that servant's servant:

> How well I might have swept his floors for ever.
> I'd ask no nights off when the bustle's over
> Enjoying so the dirt. Who's prejudiced
> Against a grimed hand when his own's quite dust,

In these lines Owen captures the superficiality of social distinction, which only operates when things are normal. Introduce
a distorting factor like imminent death, and the whole idea falls
apart. The narrator would even do the most menial tasks if he
could only live:

> I'd love to be a sweep, now, black as Town,
> Yes, or a muckman . . .

The stanza ends with him seeing himself as he is: 'Must I be
his load?' He is a load of bandages and wounds and it is a fate
he cannot alter. His hopelessness leads him in the next stanza to
even more frantic longings for any sort of life; he would even
exchange his humanity with a rat or a microbe.

> Dead men may envy living mites in cheese,
> Or good germs even. Microbes have their joys,
> And subdivide, and never come to death.

His neurotic craving for life becomes so overwhelming that he would be a microbe which, he thinks, must have 'joy' because it never actually dies. He considers exchanging what little human life he has for the vegetative 'life' of a flower, and the easiness of such a life leads him to one of Owen's few literary allusions, a reference to Shelley, who romantically imagines in death a total return to nature, 'I shall be one with nature, herb and stone'. This philosophy, however, is more succinctly put by the ordinary soldiers in their phrase 'pushing up daisies'. The poetic fancy is brought down to a level of applicability for the soldiers them-selves. From here in his imagination the narrator bequeaths his body to the earth:

> To grain, then, go my fat, to buds my sap,

and he deprecates the value even of what is left of his body

> For all the usefulness there is in soap.

His body is mere fat, mere soap. Humorously, he speculates on the enemy's making him into 'man-soup', but the edge is taken off his humour by uncertainty. War has brought such horror, that even this is possible, and to speculate upon it, and upon possible German victory, breaks off this troubling line of thought. The future, after all, does not matter for him:

> Some day, no doubt, if . . .

The end of the poem renews a note of sadness. The seemingly foolish notion that the narrator will be 'better off with the plants' because he will be in peace, is not to be mocked, he declares, and adds rather movingly:

> Don't take my soul's poor comfort for your jest.

This, after all, is a dying man and his consolation, though apparently rather banal, is to him quite genuine. A soul, in fact, is better left behind than brought into war.

> But here the thing's best left at home with friends.

This is an echo of 'Insensibility' again, where a conscience is a burden and a thinking mind best discarded. The last two lines implore the imaginary listener to detach the narrator's spirit from its necessity to be housed in what little of his body is left. He is conscious of his fears and disbeliefs and that his soul is unprepared for any existence there may be in which his body has no part. Throughout the poem there has been the continual hope for life and this has always been for the body. Realizing that his soul alone could survive, he would have it more able to stand on its own, have it able

> To do without what blood remained these wounds.

After the fact of his impending death has been faced up to, after he has laughed at the fate of his body and envied every living organism, he is faced with the inevitability of certain death, but also the possibility of a continued spiritual existence. This thought frightens him by reflecting his previous unawareness of its possibility, so the last line is as much a request to himself as it is to his listener.

This is a complex poem in which Owen explores a wider range of emotional and intellectual notions than usual. There are no descriptions of battle—only of its effect on the body and mind of one shattered survivor. It might be better addressed to the soldiers than to the ordinary reader, for it offers a difficult proposal to them by saying that in spite of the easiness of abandoning the conscience, the intellect, the feelings, the soul while at war, in the final event it is the soul that *might just* survive. The body is sure to die whether whole or maimed; the spirit, however, must be in a state of readiness, to make up.

Disabled

Basically, this is the story of a young soldier who, for all the wrong reasons, enlists in the army and when we see him a year later he has lost both his legs and part of an arm, and has lost too all the aspects of life that only a year before he had lived for. Although there is the usual sympathetic treatment of his case, Owen does not gloss over the fact that he has acted foolishly and invited many of his troubles. Yet, in the end, the sheer sense of desolation is overwhelming and Owen cannot withhold the reader's compassion for this ruined figure.

At the beginning of the poem we may well suspect that Owen is describing an old man.

> He sat in a wheeled chair, waiting for dark,
> And shivered in his ghastly suit of grey,

With nothing to look forward to, he simply waits for darkness to fall and with it sleep and the possibility of release. The second line seems to carry on the notion of his being happier in the dark by taking up his greyness—of appearance and of spirit—and linking it with 'ghastly' implying his ghostlike existence, happy at night. Further, it suggests the ghostlike quality of his life, a pale reflection of his former self. This succinct opening is highly effective and the sadness evoked by the young man's appearance is emphasized by the sound of boys' voices in the distance. The fact that children can be playing quite without care while he sits waiting for darkness is an impressionistic picture of despair—a composite achievement of suggestion and meaning and tone—which presents us with the mood of the poem. It is a very fine stanza.

The time of evening is the theme which gives a continuity into section two of the poem. At this time just a year before, the young man was about to 'go on the town'. The evening had a special magical quality which transformed the trees and the girls and the entire atmosphere. Things were never better but, Owen reminds us, that was in the past,

> In the old times, before he threw away his knees.

The effect of the second part of the line is to make us stop and question its sense, and Owen leaves us at this point to ponder what he will later make apparent. The poem does not begin to explain yet, it still concentrates on the loss and change which he has incurred by actions which we now suspect to have been not altogether outside his control:

> Now he will never feel again how slim
> Girls' waists are, or how warm their subtle hands;
> All of them touch him like some queer disease.

The feeling of total transformation could not be stronger. What he once most enjoyed is now impossible; the people who once

most fawned on him now avoid him, frightened that his disable-
ment may be contagious. Owen must be using 'subtle' here in
the sense of clever or dexterous, but there is, however, the
connotation of cunning implied by the word. Elsewhere in the
poem, we can see examples of a misogynism which recurs in
other poems.

The third section again deals with the young man's past self
and particularizes upon his physical beauty. An artist had been
obsessed by it, had been 'silly for his face', for, paradoxically, he
had then seemed even younger than his real age, which was not
much itself. But, as Owen notes by placing it conspicuously at
the end of the line, that was 'last year':

> Now, he is old; . . .
> He's lost his colour very far from here,

Again paradoxically, he is an old man, though we know that
only a year has passed. But a year's events have brought ravages,
and no artist wants to paint him now, he's 'lost his colour'. Owen
draws our attention to the distinction by using colour in a punned
sense, appropriate for an artist's view of the man. The same hint
of the voluntary nature of his ageing is given in the next line with
'poured', implying that his pouring out of his blood was somehow
a deliberate action. That it was not his intention to be maimed
we soon discover, but we also discover that his determination to
enlist was a wilful and capricious action of the worst sort.

His motives are analysed in the fourth stanza. What emerges is
that this young man has been caught up in the wave of unquestioning war hysteria; he has joined up out of self-aggrandisement, a
quest for glory; from vanity; from notions of romance; but for
no moral or conscientious reasons. At one time, says Owen, he
enjoyed a wound, but only the grazes of the football field, which
showed his masculinity and that he had played well. The blood
justified his being carried off the field 'shoulder-high'. Then he
got drunk, and in that state felt 'he'd better join'. The manly
thing to do was to enlist, and exhilarated with success and alcohol
he did so, lying to the recruitment board by advancing his age
to nineteen. That was last year and now he's an old man—at
nineteen or twenty! Now 'He wonders why'; now that he is
experienced, with no success going to his head, with time to

reflect, without his youth, he wonders why. Owen provides all the reasons but the young man must supply for himself the final answer to his question. He was driven by vanity:

> Someone had said he'd look a god in kilts,

Ironically, now he is dressed in drab grey. And he enlisted, too, to impress his girl:

> That's why; and may be, too, to please his Meg;
> Aye, that was it, to please the giddy jilts

Note the bitterness used to describe all women in this line. They are flighty, frivolous, 'giddy' and their affections do not last, they are changeable 'jilts'. Owen may merely be stressing that once his godlike appearance has altered, the women's feelings also alter, but he does it with great vehemence. To concentrate on Owen's attitude towards women throughout his poems would require a more detailed study than this guide, but certainly in this poem, he places them in an extremely pejorative light.

The attitude of the military officials also comes under criticism.

> He asked to join. He didn't have to beg;
> Smiling they wrote his lie; aged nineteen years.

The first half of the line stresses the young man's folly, but the rest censures the officials' utilization of his naïvity. They smile in disbelief, because we know from earlier in the poem that he does not even look the age he is; but he is enlisting so they have no intention of challenging his lie. Now we see that no moral scruples took him into the war:

> Germans he scarcely thought of; all their guilt,
> And Austria's, did not move him . . .

Nor did he know then what there was to fear:

> . . . And no fears
> Of Fear came yet. . . .

Fear is capitalized to make it stand out as the force to be reckoned with that he subsequently knew it to be. If any really positive feeling took him into the war, it was romance.

> . . . He thought of jewelled hilts
> For daggers in plaid socks; of smart salutes;
> And care of arms; and leave; and pay arrears;
> *Esprit de corps*; and hints for young recruits.

All the trappings of military life; all the high-blown phrases; the colour, pageantry, pomp, friendships, manliness, captured his immature imagination. Yet the reality is terribly different.

Marching off to cheers and drums, he returns to sympathy and solitude. He is visited now by a 'solemn man'—no young girls, no fellow football players, no brother soldiers.

> Only a solemn man who brought him fruits
> *Thanked* him; and then inquired about his soul.

There is no drinking now, only fruit, the traditional gift to the invalid. The man's thanks are of course meaningless to the soldier and Owen emphasizes this by italicizing the word. Finally, since the young man's body is no longer to be considered, the man 'enquires about his soul', preparing him for death.

The final stanza looks to the future which offers only 'a few sick years in Institutes', doing '. . . what things the rules consider wise'. His freedom is gone and other people will decide what is 'wise' for him to do. Similarly, in the next line:

> And take whatever pity they may dole.

They will give out charity in a formal manner and he, deprived of any option, must accept it. Very near to the end of the poem, Owen adds a tragic note:

> To-night he noticed how the women's eyes
> Passed from him to the strong men that were whole.

The young man who was once the object of female adoration is now ignored. The comment on the fickle nature of women we must mention but pass over—and feel moved by the sense of loss in the lines. If he had lost all interest in women, as they have in him, he could look on them unconcerned, but he still has the same desires, only his good looks have gone. The thought brings him back to reality. It is late and cold and he is left helpless

> How cold and late it is! Why don't they come
> And put him into bed? Why don't they come?

The passivity of his life is brilliantly stressed by Owen's mention of them putting him into bed. This man who was once fit and proud and independent can do nothing for himself. The final question is haunting and Owen may be implying by it that even the nurses and attendants feel as revolted as the girls or as disinterested as the women who merely pass their eyes over him. The transformation is absolute and it is the effect of one year in the war.

The poem takes a deeper view of the deforming nature of the war than most of the others which follow this line. We cannot overlook Owen's stressing of the willingness of this young man to involve himself in something which he did not understand. Yet for all the young man's folly, the pathos of the situation compels us to sympathize fully with him. Owen could be sanctimonious here and could blame the young man himself, but rather he blames his naïvity. A poet with less compassion might well have drawn a bitter picture of this man. But to have had so much and to have lost it is more than enough punishment for forgiveable defects, and by his continual restating of that loss, Owen emphasizes his commiseration. The final stanza does this brilliantly with the images of him now being ignored and helpless where previously he was the centre of attention.

To expand into a psychological study of such accuracy is a new departure for Owen and he brings it off with mastery. This is not just anti-war poetry, though it is that; it is poetry with width of sight, displaying penetrating accuracy into human nature of the sort our very finest poets have produced.

Mental Cases

This poignant poem follows 'Disabled' closely in style and theme but here Owen deals with mental abnormality resulting from the war. Because it is less obvious than physical deformity, it is an even less pleasant topic, but Owen was determined to cover as many of the war's effects as he could without shrinking. Though

alarming and distressing, the poem has not the scope of 'Disabled',
nor the depth of observation, but its strength lies in its ability to
capture the full effect of the war's destruction on these men in
minute detail.

It begins with the same tone as 'Disabled', and presents us with
a collection of shadows.

> Who are these? Why sit they here in twilight?
> Wherefore rock they, purgatorial shadows,

Even the 'shadows' themselves do not know who they are and
the question, though intended rhetorically, accentuates this. The
Twilight in the day, of course, merely reflects the growing darkness within their minds. To Owen, these men seem like ghosts,
trapped still on earth. They are creatures in purgatory, a place
of suffering and expiation, neither hell nor heaven. The image
of purgatory is a particularly effective one, since the men are too
insane to understand fully their own condition, but not insane
enough to be oblivious of it. The image is also used ironically
because purgatory is a place where sins are worked or suffered
away, and though these men are suffering, it is not for sins of
their own. They are suffering for the faults of all mankind.

The rest of the stanza is full of comparisons to skulls, animals and
ghosts.

> Baring teeth that leer like skulls' teeth wicked?

The word 'baring', of course, suggests an animal in a state of
fear and aggression, and we can see as the poem progresses that
these men suffer from both neurotic fear and rage. The reference
to the leer like a skull is also a re-emphasis of the deadly nature
of these living-corpses. Thinking of how they went insane, Owen
calls to mind the suffering they must all have endured, 'stroke on
stroke of pain—', but he knows that more than this was needed
to bring about such total devastation:

> . . . —but what slow panic,
> Gouged these chasms round their fretted sockets?

Panic implies an instantaneous fear and Owen would like us to
think of fear at this level of intensity, but also to imagine it
protracted over a long period, 'slow panic'. 'Gouged' implies the

violent nature of the assault upon their reason, suggesting blunt force applied to the eyes. 'Chasms' emphasizes how sunk their eyes are, and 'fretted' is used in two senses. Fretted means lined, which obviously re-emphasizes the sunken effect round their eyes, and it also means tormented, worn, distressed, all of which recall the 'slow panic' of the line before. Even through their hair, as from the palms of their hands, 'misery swelters'. 'Surely' says Owen 'we have perished', surely we are dead and in the realms of ghosts in hell. This cannot be life, such figures cannot be alive, and with the question 'who these hellish?' we are back to where the stanza began.

Stanza two attempts to answer these questions and to explain the origins of these mental cases.

> —These are men whose minds the Dead have ravished.

The memories and visions and nightmares of the dead are part of the cause. Guilt at what they have seen or been a part of has destroyed them. Owen wishes us to be quite clear about the vast numbers of dead they have seen:

> Multitudinous murders they once witnessed.
> Wading sloughs of flesh these helpless wander,

It is worth noting that Owen talks of their memories as still affecting them. They wade still (notice he uses the more active participle 'wading'), it is not all in the past; in the only functioning part of their brains they cannot choose but see visions of the 'carnage incomparable' they were once in the midst of. The words 'wading' and 'sloughs' both suggest the mire of bodies through which they passed. With dead men everywhere they cannot avoid

> Treading blood from lungs that had loved laughter.

Always before them are the sights and sounds of death on an unimaginable scale:

> Batter of guns and shatter of flying muscles,
> Carnage incomparable, and human squander
> Rucked too thick for these men's extrication.

The alliteration of the forceful t's in 'ba*tt*er' and 'sha*tt*er' embodies the sound of the event itself, and coming after a line of balanced phrase and simple diction, the polysyllables of 'carnage incomparable' arrest the reader's attention, while the image of easy availability and extravagance implied by 'human squander' completes the impression of total devastation. The final line with its alliteration

> Ru*c*ked *t*oo *t*hi*ck* for *t*hese men's ex*t*rica*t*ion

gives the impression of the corpses piling up and recalls by 'extrication' the original idea of these men being in purgatory— the place of external extrication where they work for their release.

In the third stanza, Owen goes on to describe the effect which these ever-present visions have. The most obvious cause of suffering is the guilt the men feel, emphasized here by references to blood.

> Sunlight seems a blood-smear; night come blood-black;
> Dawn breaks open like a wound that bleeds afresh.

Everything is seen in terms of blood and the perpetual torment causes their eyes to 'shrink tormented/Back into their brains'. This, says Owen, is why they look so horrific:

> —Thus their heads wear this hilarious, hideous,
> Awful falseness of set-smiling corpses.

This is why their faces are so unnatural, simultaneously appearing hideous and yet as if they were laughing. They smile like corpses, stiffly and falsely, but it is because of the corpses they always see that they look as they do. This, says Owen, is why they bare their teeth and are continually 'plucking at each other'—it is terror and guilt which drives them into emotional self-castigation.

> Picking at the rope-knouts of their scourging;

In an effort to expiate their guilt in their 'purgatory', they scourge their memories and their minds. Owen uses 'knouts' to echo knots as they try to unravel the knotted states of mind they are in, and also uses it in its ordinary meaning as whip or scourge. In their frenzy they snatch at those who pass, who, after all, like everyone involved in the war, are the actual cause of their suffering

> Pawing us who dealt them war and madness.

Owen links the war and madness as the obvious cause-and-effect they are, and in the final line he tries to pass a little of the guilt onto other people, shouldering some himself, reminding his readers that the blame is universal and that these men who suffer openly are the products of a general guilt which for them in particular is too great to live with. The final word on the mental cases, however, is 'pawing'. With its suggestion of the animalistic level to which these men have been reduced, he carries us right back to the beginning of the poem and the 'baring teeth' lines.

It is characteristic of Owen not to use these mental cases as scapegoats for the huge weight of guilt he knows must be generally shouldered. He pities them because he knows it is only as a result of enduring circumstances beyond those which any human being could be expected to endure that they are as they are. They, in fact, are responding openly in the way all of Europe should be, Owen implies—not that everyone should be mad, but that everyone should be questioning the validity of 'carnage incomparable' and how it could have been avoided.

The Chances

From the beginning the tone of 'The Chances' is one of self-assurance and resignation: confidence in the certainty of the possibilities that can befall and resignation to whatever may arise. The poem is narrated by the one soldier out of five mentioned who survives unscathed from an encounter.

The atmosphere of acceptance is evoked in the first line

> I mind as 'ow the night afore that show

where the engagement, even in retrospect, is called a 'show'. This is a slang word for a fight, but it is also associated with show used in the sense of entertainment. Though this second meaning obviously does not fit in here, the choice of the word cannot avoid recalling its wider connotations for the reader. Line two conveys the self-assurance of the men.

> Us five got talkin',—we was in the know.

But Owen destroys this at the end of the poem, when it is

forcefully brought home to them that they have not taken all possibilities into account. Their information tells them that an encounter is planned and that they are to lead it. The same feeling of acceptance of fate is continued by 'we're for it'. Even the slight resentment of the next line is hardly emphatic:

> "First wave we are, first ruddy wave; that's tore it!"

Knowing that someone must go first 'over the top', they show little real indignation that it is them. In a belief that the possibilities facing them are somehow less fearful if they are explained, one of the soldiers lists them. The terrible nature of what he is presenting is at odds with the calmness of his listing—but then Jimmy's 'seen some scrappin':

> "Ye get knocked out; else wounded—bad or cushy;
> Scuppered; or nowt except yer feelin' mushy."

That Jimmy's 'seen some scrappin' is indicative of how the soldiers approach the war. Experience has taught them resignation, so a battle becomes a 'scrap', a 'show'. Having survived longest Jimmy has analyzed the possibilities, and the chances as he sees them are not entirely daunting: apart from death and serious mutilation, there is also the possibility of emerging unharmed; or best of all, being wounded only slightly but enough to be sent home, 'blighty' as the soldiers called it.

The second part of the poem sustains this resigned tone, and just as Jimmy enumerated his possibilities, so the narrator, with equal composure lists their various fates. One soldier has been killed:

> One of us got the knock-out, blown to chops.

The line draws forth no suggestion of pity from the narrator, it is direct and matter of fact. A second is crippled, but he is disposed of with similar equanimity:

> T'other was 'urt, like, losin' both 'is props.

His crippling is reduced to a mere 'hurt'; his legs are talked of as if they had been at the time no different from the crutches he now will have, and even the hurt is governed by the word 'like' in the middle of the line. There is no emotion here. The tone of acceptance of these events as all part of war's risks is never broken. The narrator has escaped unhurt, for which he offers a perfunctory prayer, 'praise God Almighty', though if God has to have an interest in his well-being He might give him just a small wound:

> (Though next time please I'll thank 'im for a blighty.)

The fourth soldier has been taken prisoner of war, though quite how much of a 'misfortoon' this is is open to question, since the man is now out of direct line of battle and, though prisoner, is safe in the custody of Germans who are spoken of almost friendlily as 'Fritz'.

Only the assured Jim has not fitted into the sequence of predicted events. The other men have fallen for one or other of the proposed chances, and that is that, no grief no remorse, only acceptance. But Jim is 'poor young Jim', not because of his especially bad fate, but because his five possibilities have been disproved by himself. In Jim are all the five chances, and one more:

> E's wounded, killed, and pris'ner, all the lot,
> The bloody lot all rolled in one. Jim's mad.

In accounting for possibilities, Jim omitted insanity and ironically it is this which throws his predictions out. The emphasis of the stark phrase 'Jim's mad' at the end of the sentence is unmistakable. The sixth chance is not only a chance in itself, but also the sum of the others.

Owen may well be inviting us to understand the diversity of assaults war can make upon the soldiers in this poem and to consider the devastating effect of insanity, which incorporates all other wounds, but his main emphasis would appear to be on the attitude of the soldiers themselves. Complacency and acceptance fill the poem. If he is seriously expounding any theme, it is the folly of acceptance, for beneath the story of five men's fitting into a prediction, with one tragic exception, this is the more insistent note.

The Dead-Beat

While at Craiglockhart, Owen met and was deeply impressed by
Siegfried Sassoon. Though in the long-run Sassoon's style did not
influence his work, in the immediate impact of the first meeting,
Owen produced this poem which he claimed was 'something in
Sassoon's style'. Sassoon's particular style, as mentioned earlier,
is a highly ironic one, his resentment displaying itself in bitter,
scornful invective. In 'The Dead-Beat' Owen attempts to express
pity for a young man whose shell-shock is misunderstood,
initially even by Owen himself, and the young soldier dies, but
by abandoning his own somewhat melancholic, elegiac style he
loses a great deal of effect. The irony of the poem is carried too
far and the satirical dialogue seems somehow too strained.

The title of this poem casts an ambiguity on it from the
beginning. 'Dead-Beat' usually means exhausted, but it is also
slang for a worthless shirker, a scrimshanker, and it is in this
double sense that it applies to the poem. Everyone thinks the
soldier a malingerer until the end when, with his death, we
discover he was really 'dead-beat', drained of life. The ambiguity
continues in the first line, where after the quite factual 'He
dropped', we have '—more sullenly than wearily'. 'Sullenly' and
'wearily' are used together to preserve the uncertainty of response
to this man's fall. Having fallen he lies, not lifeless as in death,
but senseless, without response (a continuation of the meaning
and connotations of 'sullen'), wide-eyed but obtuse 'like a cod'.
This image is continued by the reference to the soldier being
'heavy like meat', like the dead weight of flesh without animation
or spirit. The response he provokes among those around and
from Owen is certainly not ambiguous:

> And none of us could kick him to his feet;
> Just blinked at my revolver, blearily;

There is no tenderness or sympathy—only threats and kicks. The
men kick him as they would an animal, and when this fails,
Owen threatens him with his gun, to which the response is still
the same. He blinks as if he were unable to focus on what he sees,

he is as oblivious to threats as he is to blows. The soldier is wrapped in his own thoughts and murmurs:

> 'I'll do 'em in,' he whined. 'If this hand's spared,
> I'll murder them, I will.'

The unspecified 'them' upon whom he is so determined to have revenge keeps up the ambiguity that runs throughout the poem till the final settlement. Does he refer to the enemy? Or is he thinking of someone at home? The answer is not given but Owen may be hinting at it when in the next section an unidentified onlooker mentions some possible causes for what they all take for mere cowardice.

> It's Blighty, p'raps, he sees; his pluck's all gone,
> Dreaming of all the valiant, that aren't dead:
> Bold uncles, smiling ministerially;
> Maybe his brave young wife, getting her fun
> In some new home, improved materially.
> It's not these stiffs have crazed him; nor the Hun.

Appropriately in such an ambiguous poem, the onlooker remains anonymous. His suggestions for what may have broken the soldier's spirit are figures whom Owen and all soldiers detested, the 'valiant' who were only brave by virtue of their protestations of courage, since they were well out of the war in Britain. The real valiant are the dead—these are the armchair patriots. Then he specifies some of the 'valiant'. The 'bold uncles' refers both to literal uncles and to the politicians and warmongers who can afford to smile in the safety of home. Pictures of Asquith and Lloyd-George with their Cabinets at this time will bring this image to life. Then he turns to the 'brave young wife' who may have found herself a replacement husband. 'Brave' is used sarcastically because she is deserting her husband, not bearing up to his absence. There is also an archaic use of 'brave' meaning over-bold, rather showy, and Owen may be evoking some of this shade of meaning too. Any possibility of her fidelity is shattered, as is the notion of their marriage being a deep relationship, for now she is 'getting her fun' elsewhere. Notice too how Owen uses 'In some new *home*' emphasizing the shallowness with which the word is normally used. Home for the soldiers was all they desired, but to this fickle woman it is merely a place to 'get her fun'. After the slang expressions the formality of the term 'improved materially' strikes a discord, endorsing the break that her leaving him has made. It also, of course, disparages female worth, and insinuates that she adopts the moral standards of a prostitute, going to whoever can keep her best. This is just another aspect of Owen's derogation of women. These, claims the onlooker, preying on his mind have deranged him, not the carnage or the enemy.

The next section of the poem is matter of fact. Having no other way of disposing of this unresponsive piece of flesh, they 'send him down' to the sick bay, not for his own good, but to put him 'out of the way'. The physically wounded can show their injuries but there is no compassion for the mentally injured. This is stressed by the isolated placing of 'unwounded' at the beginning of line 17. To the onlookers, and to the stretcher-bearers who wink over him, he is a shirker.

The next day the doctor appears and announces the young man's death. Striking as this announcement is in itself, Owen emphasizes it by first of all mentioning the 'Doc.'s well-whiskied laugh' and then by recording the actual words he is supposed to have said:

> 'That scum you sent last night soon died. Hooray.'

The use of 'laugh' when he is announcing a death is a condemnation; that it is a drunken laugh is a further reproach, but the words themselves are damning. That 'scum' we have only just heard was a 'stout lad . . . before that strafe'. With his mental wounding, which it is especially appalling a doctor could not understand, he ceases to be a 'good chap' and becomes 'scum'. The sense of relief and joy at his death contrast violently with the totally passive nature of the young man's despair. The active joy expressed by 'Hooray' clashes conspicuously with the 'sullen' withdrawal into himself of the soldier.

The climax throws a whole new light on to what has happened, of course, and the bitterness of the last two lines accentuates the guilt Owen feels at having been insensitive to the young man's state. The only quarrel with the ironic nature of the end of the poem is the force of the diction. Somehow it seems too overdone because no matter how callous a man was, he would hardly express such open joy at the death of anyone. The line *sounds* wrong. It does not sound like direct speech at all—coming from a doctor or not.

This apart, however, 'The Dead-Beat' is a moving poem illustrating not only the effect of the war's pressures on the soldier, but also the external forces, the suspicions and resentments at those left at home. It also displays how, though the war may cause some men to withdraw totally into themselves, as in the case of the soldier, it can also deprive even the most apparently sensitive men of their humanity for a time. The 'well-whiskied' doctor is not the only one who is guilty. The guilt is shared among those who tried to kick him up, and with Owen himself. Perhaps the one to bear least blame is the onlooker who, though he doubted the genuineness of the soldier's state, at least saw some reasons for it. He showed at least a degree of understanding, if not sympathy. The overall effect of the poem must be this alarming warning, that war is so destructive that it can crush the humanity not just from the common soldiers, but even from a man of Owen's sensitivity.

S.I.W.

As the title suggests (S.I.W. is an abbreviation for Self-Inflicted Wound), this is a poem which describes physical injury self-inflicted by a young soldier after months of suffering. His suffering is not all physical, however, unlike many of the soldiers already encountered—and it might be noted that Owen ranges through all classes and types—for this man's struggle is largely within him as he tries to live up to empty phrases and follow hollow creeds. The poem is in four sections. Section I sets the scene, and provides us with the background to the young man's action by showing us his life just prior to his joining up and contrasting it with the reality of war. Section II is 'The Action', the young man's suicide. Section III, entitled 'The Poem', provides a more dignified explanation of his action in a 'poetic' idiom. Section IV is a brief 'epilogue' or postscript, adding a final ironic touch.

Section I begins with the soldier's leaving home. It is a middle-class home where 'traditional' values are upheld and in which people behave along predictably regular lines. What they are

seeing off is a mere 'lad', yet they instruct him to 'show the Hun
a brave man's face'. Perhaps this is the basic cause of all that
happens. From the outset this *boy* is expected to act like a *man*—
and a brave man—to be something in effect which he is quite the
antithesis of. Notice the middle-class ring of 'Father' stuck
prominently at the beginning of the third line. Without a pronoun
or an adjective to qualify it, without making it 'his' or 'their'
father, but by leaving it blankly 'Father', the word assumes the
disconcerting overtones of the genteel family where the husband
is 'father' and his wife is 'mother'. The childish dependence on
father is stressed in the line too:

> Father would sooner him dead than in disgrace,—
> Was proud to see him going, aye, and glad.

The unreal cliché that his father would rather have his son dead
than a coward soon comes home to this family (though it is
carefully concealed from them) in a forceful way. The impression
that the boy is going off to fight simply because it is what young
men of his class do, and purely to please his family, is heightened
by:

> Perhaps his mother whimpered how she'd fret
> Until he got a nice safe wound to nurse.

The word 'whimpered' suggests the smallness, the demureness,
of the woman's emotions. She does not sob or wail or even stay
straightfaced. She whimpers, mouselike, afraid of open emotions.
She will 'fret', another word suggesting the diminutive nature of
her feelings, until the boy is wounded—not badly but 'safely' and
'nicely' so that he may be sent home but they will know that he
'did his bit' and can display the wound as a trophy to friends.
Very soon their son realizes that wounds are neither 'nice' nor
'safe'. Appropriately, his sisters wish they too could go off to
assume manly, soldierly attitudes; for to them soldiering is the
striking up of poses—shooting, charging, cursing. Their lack of
understanding of what awaits their brother is distressing. His
brothers do what they think will assist him—send him cigarettes,
and the whole family will write regularly to their 'lad' who is
fighting for his King and Country.

The awful contrasting reality of the war appears in the second half of this section. Unaware of his true condition, his family believe the reassurances of his safety which he gives them in his letters (cf. 'The Letter') and write to him accordingly. He writes on the butt of his gun, tormented by the bullets which fly past him occasionally. If the bullets were frequent, he might be able to take cover. But they are spasmodic enough for him to outface, yet frightening enough to slowly wear him down:

> And misses teased the hunger of his brain.
> His eyes grew old with wincing, and his hand
> Reckless with ague. . . .

The slow erosion of his nerves is conveyed in an expressive simile which draws on the trench life for its point of comparison:

> . . . Courage leaked, as sand
> From the best sand-bags after years of rain.

This is perhaps more arresting coming after the rather too quaint 'ague' for infirmities in the first part of the line. Notice the effective placing of 'best' in the middle of the line. As we know, this is a young man of 'good' background, but like the sand-bags which cannot resist the continual force of the weather, he cannot endure the nervous strain of trench life. However, he has further troubles for within him are still the remnants of the urges to 'duty' made upon him by his family and his upbringing.

> But never leave, wound, fever, trench-foot, shock,
> Untrapped the wretch. . . .

No reminder of the pleasantness of home, no suffering, no disease, no fear could 'untrap' this lad. He is caught by his own futile beliefs that he is 'doing the right thing'. The banality of high-sounding phrases has never been put to the test for him before, and now he cannot see through the words to the reality and behave accordingly. Death may be wished for but it does not come. He must suffer torture, brought about by 'this world's Powers . . . run amok'. The values he supports are, ironically, the very causes of his suffering.

Owen breaks the section here and after the gap touches on a new theme of inflicting a 'Blighty' wound, serious enough to ship him home. He knows others have done it secretly, and the idea attracts him.

> He'd seen men shoot their hands, on night patrol.
> Their people never knew. Yet they were vile.

Notice that he is discouraged from pursuing the idea by the thought of his family. Though they would not know, he would still feel he was letting them down. The middle-class ethos is once again stressed by 'their people', with its public-school ring. His dismissal of them has a similar ring and a note of this merely being a blanket phase, a public-school expression of disapproval, the application of which can cover anything, 'they were vile'. He is supported still by the void phrases of his upbringing:

> 'Death sooner than dishonour, that's the style!'
> So Father said.

The last tag, 'So Father said', is slipped in by Owen but it shows how little this man thinks independently. And so we are back to the beginning and the basic fallacy of sending out 'a boy' to be 'a man'.

We do not see the action taking place. We are only with the patrol who find him. At first there is an uncertainty about his death.

> One dawn, our wire patrol
> Carried him. This time, Death had not missed.
> We could do nothing but wipe his bleeding cough.

Only with the next line do we realize what has happened:

> Could it be accident?—Rifles go off . . .
> Not sniped? No. . . .

The dots after 'off' are to indicate a pause while the embarrassed patrol try to find a suitable cover up for the obvious suicide; '(Later they found the English ball.)' is the final proof. It is again ironic that Owen should stress the '*English* ball', for here was a lad supporting all the traditional values of middle-class English life. Taking his life with an English bullet seems an added rebuke.

Section III, headed 'The Poem', explains the deeper causes of the soldier's actions. These are brilliantly summed up in the first line

> It was the reasoned crisis of his soul

The line echoes the phrase in 'Mental Cases', 'slow panic'. The linking of 'crisis', with its associations of immediacy, with 'reasoned' which suggests thought-out, produces the same off-setting effect. The intensity of the crisis is there but instead of being short-lived it is lingering. The future offering only slavery to the guns, and tears, and captivity within the confining trench —metaphorically described as a house 'curtained with fire, roofed in with creeping fire', not a fire to consume him immediately, but a 'slow grazing fire, that would not burn him whole'—was sufficient to drive him wild with torment. This continual baiting with the lure of death as a release that does not come has driven him to suicide. The actuality of the war has triumphed over the hollow patriotic phrases.

Section IV is only two lines long, yet it is a perfect postscript to the poem. The soldier is buried with the gun he has used to take his life—note the word 'kissed' indicating the pleasure that his suicide has been to him—and in composing a letter to his mother they have been able to tell a literal truth that her son had 'died smiling'. He has died with an apparent grin but it is his open-mouthed 'kissing' of the gun and the grin is a maniac one. For the parents, however, there is consolation. As far as they know, their son played his part and died honourably. What is sad perhaps is that they are allowed to remain in their state of ignorant content. We feel that if they had known they might have been shocked into thinking. But more true to life is the devised message.

This is a sad poem not because a young man dies at the end of it, but because the lad need not have died at all. A product of his class—and Owen is *by no means* using this poem as an attack on class structure in Britain, he had a far more urgent task in hand—the boy is trapped into accepting a pattern of behaviour that in no way equips him for life as he has to live it. Under these circumstances he is tragically destined to end as he does. The message of the poem is not addressed to the boy. He is largely helpless by the point at which we see him. It is to 'Father' and 'Mother', for it was they who created and styled him for this unavoidable fate.

Smile, Smile, Smile

This is thought to have been Owen's last poem, written on 23 September 1918. The title is an ironic application of the line from the most popular song of the war 'Pack up your troubles in your old kitbag and smile, smile, smile'. The men Owen describes have no reason to smile at all, for they see desolation around them, with no hope of release offered and empty jingoism at home.

Right from the beginning we are left in no doubt as to the men's real condition. They are bedraggled and demoralized:

> Head to limp head, the sunk-eyed wounded scanned
> Yesterday's *Mail*; . . .

They cluster round for support as much as to share one paper. Their condition contrasts markedly with the phoney brightness of the newspaper reports. British casualties are reported but not made a centre of attention, they are 'typed small', while the enemy's defeats are exaggerated in a sensational headline: 'Vast Booty from our Latest Haul.' All the words of the headline are melodramatic: 'vast' implying an almost inconceivable hugeness; 'booty' implies plunder to be divided among everyone; 'haul' suggests captured spoils, and the 'our' placed quite unobtrusively in the middle creates a sense of solidarity between 'our' troops and 'our' nation. A typically stirring headline, and one which heralds further empty sensationalism. The article talks of the promise of 'Cheap Homes'—homes fit for heroes—but the promise is shattered because the homes, though theoretically to be, are 'not yet planned' even. The hope is overshadowed by the needs of the war, a war which even late in 1918, was thought to be only just beginning:

> Meanwhile their foremost need is aerodromes,
> It being certain war has but begun.

The men need the end of the war, not its prolongation. Peace is deferred out of a pretence of respect and concern for the already dead rather than for the suffering living:

> Peace would do wrong to our undying dead,—
> The sons we offered might regret they died
> If we got nothing lasting in their stead.

By prolonging the war the number of 'undying dead' increases daily, and following the newspaper's spurious logic to its conclusion the war would go on forever. The dead, of course, are beyond right or wrong, but the living are not, though they are not consulted. Empty words and national pride keep the whole process in destructive momentum. The almost humorous effect of line 10 cannot be missed; it is as if the men who have been killed will be glad to have died if the war is a British Victory. Owen ironically implies that they might possibly regret their deaths regardless of the eventual outcome of the war—if the dead can be considered as able to express any feelings at all. The sons are 'offered'; they are sacrifices. From the tone of the poem, we know that they are not sacrificed to any good cause, but to vanity and militaristic pride. They are traded for national victory, swapped as the price of triumph:

> If we got nothing lasting in *their* stead.

Owen increases the quite obvious irony of the poem as it progresses. In line 14 he talks of 'We rulers sitting in this ancient spot', a phrase which recalls the blatant, strident patriotism of Shakespeare's 'This ancient seat of kings . . . this England' speech, whereas the concern that the 'rulers' may be threatened is voiced hesitantly in line 12:

> We must be solidly indemnified.

This protection is to be gained only by the loss of a whole generation. Even though the 'glory' of the action is squarely attributed to the dead, there is a tone of selfishness in these lines:

> 'We rulers sitting in this ancient spot
> Would wrong our very selves if we forgot
> The greatest glory will be theirs who fought,
> Who kept this nation in integrity.'

The phrase 'wrong *our very selves*' suggests the intrinsic selfishness of the situation in which many men must be 'offered' to make up for the militarism of the 'rulers sitting in this ancient spot'. Notice the effect of 'sitting' which implies the inactiveness of the selfish 'rulers'. They do not care how much they wrong the 'poor things' who are huddled around this newspaper, they care for their own opinions. That there was no glory in the war is Owen's major theme, that there was no 'integrity' behind it was one of his many others. To salve their consciences the 'rulers' invent a supposed righteousness to justify their actions. To its advocates, this is not a war to settle the question of economic and military supremacy, and to permit the pursuit of unhampered imperialism. It is a struggle to assert freedom and independence. Owen knew better and saw it in its true light and so he satirizes the supporters of the 'justified war' by holding up their empty phrases as a counterbalance to his down-to-earth, sordid reality.

The hollowness of the patriotic phrases of the newspaper is highlighted by the lines immediately following the report:

> . . . The half-limbed readers did not chafe
> But smiled at one another curiously
> Like secret men who know their secret safe.

Physically broken, the men are not angered by the report they have read, but cynically amused. They know the real truth, and, aware that this is a truth that only the experienced will understand, they smile because they share a secret together. They know that in spite of what the rulers may claim, most of England—meaning the English youth—is quite literally in France, and that in France they have been killed:

> Not many elsewhere now, save under France.

Ironically, these smiles of cynicism and despair are photographed and appear in British papers like the one they have just been reading, and are taken as smiles of happiness. The people who see the pictures, again ironically, are people with 'real feeling' for the soldiers, but they trust the patriotic columns and, backed up with what appears to be happy men in the photographs, they look no deeper. But Owen does not lay any blame on them, it is the whole system; so the men may as well go on and Smile, Smile, Smile.

This is not a poem that stimulates much sense of involvement,

Like the men, Owen seems to have a cynicism which is sufficiently incapacitating to prevent the poem from having any deeper appeal than this satirical sketch expresses. He is not too ironic or at all too bitter in his attack, he simply seems resigned to accept the situation as inevitable. The only rhetoric in the poem is the void patriotic oratory of the newspaper. Perhaps aptly, the poem is written in conventional rhyming with no jarring half-rhymes, no violent images and no striking figures of speech. It evokes pity, but it is a more intellectual pity than usual, it is pity that accompanies, indeed depends upon, the acceptance of this vaguely cynically amusing picture of self-deception. Owen is almost stepping out of the situation and shaking his head in sufferance at the whole thing. This may not be a bitter poem but it is not a cheerful or optimistic one. Its message is of deception, voluntary and involuntary, all along the line by soldiers, politicians and ordinary people. The soldiers are content to keep their secret safe; the politicians happy to churn out unrealizable promises and empty speeches, and the public willing to express pity at what they believe to be the soldiers' smiling through it all. The poem offers no glimmer of hope that this situation may change; on the contrary, there is a gloom here that is more depressing than any bloody account of battle or its effects.

Inspection

Here is a dramatic indictment of the whole human race for its hypocrisy and an effort by Owen to place guilt where it belongs. The poem deals with hypocrisy throughout, from the ridiculous inspection ceremony with its final charge and punishment in the middle of the trenches, to the young having to pay for the guilt of the old.

The poem opens arrestingly with the exclamation, ' "You!" ' At once our attention is focused onto the scene which the first four lines sum up vividly. A soldier on inspection parade has appeared with dirt on his uniform. Unable to explain that it is a spot of his own blood, he is charged for the offence. The section begins sharply, in direct speech, and ends abruptly with the soldiers being dismissed. In four lines there are three questions, to two of which no answer can be attempted for the sergeant's sharp ' "'Old yer mouth" '. Notice the number of verbs with violent associations that Owen uses, 'rapped', "Old', 'snapped' and 'dismiss'. The soldier's uncertain reply, with a comma giving a pause between each word, is the slowest part of this rapid section: ' "Please, sir, it's—" '.

The next four lines, after the break in the verse, go at a slower pace, and in them Owen, accentuating the charge and punishment by placing them in quotes, brings out the ludicrousness of the situation.

> Some days 'confined to camp' he got,
> For being 'dirty on parade'.

The irony of being 'dirty' in the middle of mud-filled trenches is clear, for how could he reasonably be otherwise? Similarly, the punishment is meaningless for him since in the conditions he could be nowhere else but 'confined to camp'. At this point, however, the poem takes on a new slant as we are told that the spot on the uniform was blood, to which Owen replies factually, ' "Well, blood is dirt" '. With the notion of blood being dirt, blood loses its real meaning and becomes a symbol of guilt. We have to emphasize this as one of Owen's few literary allusions, to *Macbeth* where (in Act V, sc 1) Lady Macbeth, sleepwalking, says; 'Out damnèd spot' when the guilt she is feeling causes her to see imaginary blood on her hands. The use of an identical phrase accentuates this transference of meaning.

In the second part of the poem this image of blood is developed further. The young man, on repeating Owen's statement 'blood's dirt', makes the logical deduction that

> 'The world is washing out its stains,'. . . .

So much blood is being shed that it appears that the dirt (which blood is said to be) is to be washed out like a stain from clothes, and that by so doing, the shame of the stain will be erased. The hypocrisy of the situation in which the world's guilt has to be expunged by the death of its youth recalls 'The Parable of the Old Man and the Young' or the deception behind 'The Send-Off'.

> 'It doesn't like our cheeks so red:
> Young blood's its great objection.'

Red cheeks are—by continuing the analogy—guilty cheeks and so they have to be bled till they are white, and the whiteness suggests death:

> 'But when we're duly white-washed, being dead,
> The race will bear Field-Marshall God's inspection.'

The phrase 'white-washed' does not only apply to their white corpses, but more effectively shows the superficiality of the situation. To white-wash is merely to cover up with cleanness, to impose a surface of brightness on a much darker base. The expurgation of guilt, like the white-wash, will only be a surface cleaning; below it will be all the iniquity of the war and its promoters. It may, of course, allude to Christ's dismissal of the Pharisees as 'Whitened sepulchres'. The statesmen who began or continue the war, and all who hope to see national guilt purged by it are, like the Pharisees, hypocrites. The 'sepulchres' referring to dead and to tombs would also apply. Certainly, the image is effective because of its width of application.

The final line recalls the inspection which began the poem. Always there is a superior power, officers have superiors and God is above all. In the final 'inspection', the last judgement, no one who has guilt will escape—the whole race may be as helpless to reply at that inspection as the young soldier was at the beginning.

It must be noted that this poem relies heavily for its imagery and impact on religious allusions. The existence of an omnipotent God who will judge the world and dispense justice without bias or regard is a central premise. The sacrifice of the youth of Europe is another prevalent image, with its relation to the use of blood in such acts. Sin, suggested through dirt, and its expurgation through sacrificial bloodshed also relates heavily to religious doctrines. Altogether, the poem's success depends on an appreciation of these allusions. What consolation it offers by way of threatened judgement for the hypocrites and the guilty is only valid if a belief in God as judge and dispenser of justice is held by its readers. Without this belief the cynical effect of the poem is doubled.

As an expression of the futility of the war's rituals which are themselves merely part of the larger futility of the world's self-purification through horrific sacrifice, the poem is dramatically

effective. Told in a straightforward, quite 'unpoetic' way, it is a
striking example of Owen's ability to penetrate right to the
essence of the war. He leaves the details of how the soldier
sustained his wound aside and does not ever mention the trench
conditions. The vivid style, made immediate here by direct
speech and direct reasoning, serves as an ideal vehicle for his
acute poem.

The Calls

This is a poem about writing poetry. Its theme is Owen's struggle
in searching for an inspiring theme for his poems. He touches on
several possibilities during the seven stanzas, but not until the
last two, and more definitely the last one, does he alight upon a
theme which offers him an irresistible call. Much in the first five
stanzas of this poem appears crude and unfinished and it is in
the last two that the more familiar sympathetic Owen tone
emerges, with the last stanza itself as a sort of explanation of why
he writes that reminds us of 'Apologia Pro Poemate Meo'.

In the first stanza he considers the call of the factory siren but
decides against this subject. The final line may seem rather glib,
'But I'm lazy, and his work's crazy' but it should be borne in
mind that this was during the war, and it is almost certain that
the man in the poem was going to work if not in an armaments
factory itself, then in some branch of the 'war effort'. Owen's view
of the continuation of the war being insanity accords with the
apparently flippant line. It would be absurd, though, to claim
that this is a good stanza for the tired simile 'helpless as a pawn'
does nothing to enhance what little meaning emerges from the
man's being '. . . pushed and drawn/Backwards and forwards'
for no apparent reason. What the stanza does convey, however,
is that the notion of 'The Dignity of Labour' does not have any
appeal to Owen as a subject for a poem. There is no dignity in
this man's 'crazy' work.

Stanza two goes back to childhood with the ringing of an aptly
high-pitched, 'treble' bell. Here the same faults appear, the
images of a schoolboy 'pulling up his sock' or of the schoolgirl 'in
the inky frock' are too worn to have any striking effect. As in the
earlier stanza, however, the kernel comes in the last line, with

Owen's statement that to learn from life, from nature, is a better method than relying on formal education.

> I must be crazy; I learn from the daisy.

He dismisses the possibility of writing a poem on the necessity of education.

The next stanza brings us to religion, and here too Owen finds no source of poetic inspiration in the church's dismal formality. The bell is 'stern', it 'annoys' the birds; the verger formally shuts the doors, and the implication of the excluding nature of religion is expressed. This service is for the believing within, it is not going out to anyone already uninaugurated. The organ 'moans' amen, and Owen's picture of religion is completed. The final line of this stanza harks back to that of the previous one

> Sing my religion's—same as pigeons'.

Apart from the rather silly use of coarse rhyme with 'religion's' and 'pigeons'', the theme is again a reverting to nature. Just as he found no appeal in the virtues of formal education, so formal religion does not create a response.

The fourth stanza takes us nearer to the military scene than the earlier ones. The violence of this environment is expressed in the first line where the bulges are 'blatant' and 'tear' his afternoon tranquillity. The soldiers are no less crass, and in the description of them Owen may or may not be intending to be as amusing as the scene is:

> Out clump the clumsy Tommies by platoons,

The alliteration of the 't' and 'l' sounds emphasizes their heaviness, and the use of 'Tommies' for soldiers suggests their boyish inexperience. The new soldiers try to learn marching by practising to rag-time tunes while Owen, who had passed this training, sits and looks on. The amusing or ridiculous aspects of army life provide no call for him to satirical verse.

The same disinterest in satirical poetry emerges from the picture in stanza five of the 'gold tusked' 'food hog' eating well at a time of national crisis. No mere bread for him, he has the 'more luxurious rusk'. The gourmet feeding off no doubt illicit food is drawn in terms that display Owen's disgust:

> I see a food-hog whet his gold-filled tusk

'Food-hog', comparing him to a pig who lives for eating, since food is an integral part of his name, as stressed by the hyphen; and 'gold-filled tusk', the tusk of which continues the hog image, while the gold-filled notion jars our imagination into visualizing an over-refined pig with gold-filled teeth. But Owen does not pause to apply more biting satire. This subject is not interesting enough.

Stanza six approaches the theme that Owen finds not only a call, but an irresistible demand, namely the situation of the soldiers. Hearing the sound of gunnery-practice, his nerves are shaken, recalling the bombardment of the trenches with its 'siren-shrieks' and 'crumps'. The very sound constricts his senses, 'till my small heart thumps'. His heart may be made small with fear only or he may be stressing the smallness of one person against the whole vast monstrosity of the war. But this is only an introduction to his final stanza.

Stanza seven begins with the imaginative two lines in which he claims to have heard the sighs of the soldiers in the trenches. Conscious of these men having no ability to speak for themselves, Owen feels that he must use his eloquence to help them.

> I heard the sighs of men, that have no skill
> To speak of their distress, no, nor the will!

Owen, having both the desire and the ability required—'wisdom was mine and I had mastery'—cannot resist this appeal to him.

> A voice I know. And this time I must go.

The emphasis of 'must go' creates the sense of his writing being compelled. The singular 'A voice' makes the plea all the more moving, even though we know it is the collective voice of many. The final stanza is immediately reminiscent of a passage in a letter which Owen wrote to his mother in October 1918:

> I came out here in order to help these boys—directly by leading them . . . indirectly by watching their sufferings that I may speak of them as a pleader can.[1]

[1] *Letters*, p. 580.

Here Owen's sense of purpose is outlined in prose. It is typical of him that no conventional topic should inspire him to write, neither social nor religious nor moral nor satirical sources appeal to him, only the intensity of human suffering does. This is as good an explanation of why he writes as is ever given by him. The voice is a human one, not abstract or theoretical, and to a human voice he cannot choose, he 'must go', he must speak 'as a pleader can'.

At a Calvary near the Ancre

In this poem Owen expresses his hatred not for religion, but for the church which taught that the war was a righteous war and that God favoured the British participation in it. In common with many soldiers, and many war poets, Owen saw the essential falseness of this belief. As we know from his letters and from earlier poems, he was more impressed by the pacifist teachings of Christ, whose statement: 'Greater love hath no man than this, that he lay down his life for a friend', impressed itself tremendously upon him. Like other poets too, he was aware that by his participation in the war he was breaking Christ's command, and yet being there he was unable to do anything. Consequently, the promoters of the just war belief come under a bitter, rhetorical attack in this poem.

The title itself is arresting. Owen chooses an area of the battle-field, near Ancre, and calls it Calvary, thereby associating it with the scene of Christ's crucifixion. It is a place of death, of sacrifice, the place of the skull. He sustains this image in the first line of the poem itself by referring to the roadside crosses which appear so frequently on the Continent and also by making a passing reference to 'where shelled roads part': *cross*-roads. The first stanza is really very concise and packed with expressions of double meaning. A crucifix stands at every cross-roads and one has been shattered at this spot 'In this war He too lost a limb'. The cross is alone with no other figures around it and the soldiers must satisfy themselves with this broken image as an object of their devotion:

> But His disciples hide apart;
> And now the Soldiers bear with Him.

This is the most superficially obvious meaning of the stanza, but its real meaning requires that we read a metaphorical significance into the words

> In this war He too lost a limb,

At once it evokes a unity with the soldiers. 'He too' couples the sufferings of Christ and the soldiers together. This is protracted further if for 'lost a limb' we understand Christ to have lost part of his 'body', part of his church. The soldiers are detached from the church, since they cannot reconcile its teachings with what they see around them and what they know Christ to have said, and Christ also is divorced from the church because his actual pronouncements are ignored by the clergy to support an unjustifiable situation. Having lost this 'limb', as at the original betrayal scene, the disciples have fled, the clergy now 'hide apart' from Christ's teachings. By comparing the religious leaders in this stanza to the disciples, Owen emphasizes that Christ was betrayed by a disciple, and so we become conscious by the analogy of how it is the professed supporters who betray and desert. Now the soldiers must suffer without consolation, they must 'bear with Him' the distress caused by the clergy having left Christ's teachings. The expression 'bear with' is used in the double sense of to suffer and to accept with resignation. The soldiers must do both as Christ must suffer unaided.

In the second stanza, Owen raises the intensity of his attack by changing his analogy for the clergy. This time he compares them not to the disciples who betray and desert, but to the Scribes and Pharisees who hounded Christ and pressed for his execution. The comparison is easy because Owen is attacking one set of religious leaders by direct likening to another set of similar officials. The unconcern of the Pharisees for the dying Christ is obvious—'Near Gologotha strolls many a priest'. By his having made the roadside crucifix near Ancres 'Calvary' in stanza one, the reference to Gologotha here causes the reader to see the allusion not merely to the Israel of Christ's day but to the contemporary situation of the soldiers. As the priests scorned Christ's death then, so religious leaders scorn his teaching now and scorn the men's sufferings which are directly identified with Christ's. The faces of the priests now as then are marked with pride, which Owen claims to be the mark of the devil, 'the Beast/By whom the gentle Christ's denied'. The 'mark of the beast' is an allusion to the Bible, to St John's *Revelation*, Chapter 13, Verse 16:

> And he causeth all, both small and great, rich and poor, free and bond, to receive a mark in their right hand, or in their foreheads.

The mark of the devil, the antithesis of the *gentle* Christ, is upon the priests, and it is the mark of pride.

In the third stanza, Owen also attacks the writers who urge total unquestioning obedience to the state—those who promote duty before conscience and loyalty in spite of righteousness. The Scribes were a further branch of the Jewish religious system and so the reference to official religious leaders is continued.

> The scribes on all the people shove
> And brawl allegiance to the state,

The violent overtones of 'shove' and 'brawl' are unmistakable, and the paradox of a situation where those who are supposed to be promoting peace are 'shoving' and 'brawling' their followers into an acceptance of war is strikingly significant. The 'greater love' dictum of Christ is forgotten in this 'brawl' as private consciences are 'shoved' into loyal conformity. The true followers of Christ, says Owen, *say* nothing but *act* upon Christ's teachings none the less.

> But they who love the greater love
> Lay down their life; they do not hate.

This is a poem of great bitterness but the bitterness does not rise as an insurmountable intrusion between the poem and the reader. In the middle stanza there is rhetoric but it is not too overwhelming to direct the reader away from the poem's insistent theme. The conciseness of the first stanza is especially striking and the gradual broadening of the poem's attack is a strong feature. The quiet ending embodies the resolute sincerity of 'they who love the greater love'.

Le Christianisme

This short poem continues the theme expressed in the last one, but instead of making an attack on the clergy, it assaults the church's deliberate detachment from reality. Again, it is not Christ's teachings which are challenged for, as the first line shows, a distinction is drawn between the real Christ and the 'church Christ'.

A church has been destroyed by bombardment and Owen, considering its statues and plaster saints, compares this artificiality with the essential message of Christ which all this purports to express

> So the church Christ was hit and buried
> Under its rubbish and its rubble.

There is a strong suggestion that just as the statue of Christ is encased in rubble, so the doctrines of Christ have been buried out of reach below piles of cant. The rest of the church's statues are all packed away safely in the cellars, and Owen draws an analogy between the shutting up of the statue-saints and the church's shutting itself off from the soldiers' situation, its remaining deliberately silent at a point where it should be preaching Christ's message of peace.

> In cellars, packed-up saints lie serried,
> Well out of hearing of our trouble.

The phrase 'packed-up' applied to the saints adds just a touch of bitterness on Owen's part; not only is the church deliberately isolated, but, under its piles of doctrinal 'rubbish', it may well be useless. Notice, too, that though the saints may wish to help the soldiers, they cannot, they have been well packed away— for their own safe-keeping, not for the soldiers' benefit.

The second stanza is not so immediate or as succinct in its impact. Seeing a statue of the Virgin, uninjured in the shelling, 'still immaculate' with an old tin hat as a halo, Owen thinks of how this statue, and the church it represents, cannot withstand the forces of evil pressing in on it.

> She's halo'd with an old tin hat,
> But a piece of hell will batter her.

The disconcerting note in the stanza is in its second line, however.

> One Virgin still immaculate
> Smiles on for war to flatter her.

It would appear that the statue expects to be complimented and made much of by the war. Even without a comparison to the church, the idea of a sinless saint being concerned over flattery is unusual. The comparison to the church, of course, is that it should be remaining true to its founder's teachings, but it is not. Its perfect image is being as much corrupted as the Virgin's because it is using the war to reassert its own position in spite of Christ's teachings of pacificism. Like the statue, Owen believes the church cannot be 'flattered' and yet escape unharmed; just as the statue will be damaged so with the church, 'a piece of hell will batter her'. After the war, the church's hypocrisy will rebound and it will lose face all the more when it comes to unpacking the 'packed-up saints'.

The first stanza of this poem quite brilliantly sums up the attitude of a hypocritical religion in lines 3 and 4, and though the second stanza has not quite this edge of impact, it makes an analogous comparison that cannot be overlooked. Though short, the poem is not without bite.

Soldier's Dream

This is a strange little poem which tells of the dashing of a soldier's dream on his waking to find that all his weapons are in reality intact, whereas in the dream they had been destroyed. The destruction of the weapons, by Christ, is a passive one. Notice the lack of violent action in the words 'fouled', 'buckled with a smile', 'rusted . . . with His tears'. The weapons—which we know from other poems, 'The Last Laugh' and 'Arms and the Boy', represent more the deadliness of the war than the enemy—are made incapable of working out of kindness in the first stanza, and the beginning of the second offers a promise of the end of the war:

And there were no more bombs, of ours or Theirs,
Not even an old flint-lock, nor even a pikel.

The diminutive 'pikel', which sounds rather absurd, is probably used to show the extent of Christ's ban on weapons, from the smallest to the largest. This vision of peace, however, is broken for 'God was vexed, and gave all power to Michael' and the soldier wakes and, finding all weapons still operable, assumes that Michael has 'seen to our repairs'.

The odd factor in the poem is that there appears to be a rift between the 'kind Jesus' of the first stanza and the vexed God of the second. The only explanation can be that Owen sees Christ's essentially revolutionary policy of peace being overthrown by the vengeful Old Testament God who urged the retributive laws of 'an eye for an eye', etc. The angel Michael is the soldier angel and as emissary of God, seems leagued against the pacific Christ. This dichotomy is rather unusual and apart from the Old Testament, vengeful God and the New Testament, pacific Christ balance, explanation is rather difficult. Certainly this is not an important poem. It is only a 'Dream' after all, but it is unusual for Owen to present us with anything so inexplicable.

Sonnet

On Seeing a Piece of Our Artillery Brought into Action

This sonnet, inspired by the sight of a huge gun being set up, deals with the question of what the future holds for those who survive the war. It is aptly placed near the end of Owen's war poems because it looks to a future which can only be bright if some vast 'gun' is directed at the human weaknesses of arrogance and resentment which Owen sees as the principal causes of war.

The image of the gun at the beginning of the poem is of a 'long black arm', threatening and heavy. It is slowly lifted up and 'towers' towards heaven. The slow rhythm of the lines suggest the sheer weight of, and the awe created by, the gun. Its every noise is a 'curse', but Owen would like to see the curse redirected and focused upon 'that Arrogance which needs thy harm', the

pride that must be backed by impressive militarism. Its every
shot should be a mere rehearsal of what it will do to blast away
national pride. The curses will not be made lightly, for this is a
blasting weapon:

> . . . rehearse
> Huge imprecations like a blasting charm!

The assault on arrogance needs a vast weapon for it is no small
vice, especially nationalistic arrogance:

> Reach at that Arrogance which needs thy harm,
> And beat it down before its sins grow worse;

The word 'beat' suggests that no gentle pressure will have effect,
and this idea is carried through to the end of the octave:

> Spend our resentment, cannon,—yea, disburse
> Our gold in shapes of flame, our breaths in storm.

The sestet brings a consideration of those who harbour no
hatred into the poem. The mood changes with the 'Yet . . .'.
It is typical of Owen to remember that not all of humanity is in
need of violent change. When the gun's effect has been achieved,
it must not be kept:

> Be not withdrawn, dark arm, thy spoilure done,
> Safe to the bosom of our prosperity.

To keep a weapon as potentially dangerous as this metaphorical
gun is as great a threat as the vices it has been used to banish.
It must be destroyed:

> But when thy spell be cast complete and whole,
> May God curse thee, and cut thee from our soul!

The overall effect is a fairly optimistic one. A great weapon may
be needed to rid humanity of its corrupting features, but at least
they can be eradicated, they are not an essentially intrinsic part
of human nature. Though his optimism was proved wrong in the
event of history, Owen's view is still a brighter one than the
circumstances might have merited.

As a poem this is not such a successful piece, mainly because

Owen places an archaic and difficult diction between his reader
and his meaning. The basic metaphorical notion of a spiritual
'gun' to beat out all the vices of humanity is not difficult to
comprehend, but couched in language such as 'imprecations',
which is a synonym for the more straightforward 'curse', and
'malism' which is an archaic word for the same, with 'spoilure'
which is Owen's own coinage, is erecting not an insurmountable
barrier, but an irksome one. The use of 'thee' and 'thou' may
have been employed to give the sonnet a biblical tone but it does
not succeed. Altogether, the piece has a phoneyness about it.
Owen can express ideas of greater complexity than this when he
wishes, but the most direct approach is usually the most successful.
Here the serious tone, with much declamation, 'yea' and 'Our
gold in shapes of flame, our breaths in storm', is all too over-done.
The last line is positively petty in its mock-rhetoric:

'May God curse thee, and cut thee from our soul!'

Technically, the poem is one of Owen's most artificial. This is
not to say that a great notion is buried under a bad delivery, but
merely that when Owen is sincere and unpretentious he can make
a simple idea come alive with sympathy and humanity. When he
is not, as here, he creates no real effect whatsoever.

The Next War

It must not be assumed that Owen was somehow being prophetic
when he wrote this poem. He could have had no idea that twenty
years after the end of the First World War, there would be
another of equally appalling proportions. At the time of his death,
though armistice was only a week away, he was quite unaware of
the proximity of the end of the war. The peace arrangements set
out in the Treaty of Versailles had not yet been drafted and the
Nazi party was not even in existence. 'The Next War' does not
anticipate all that subsequently occurred, in fact it rather
innocently underestimates the impact of the First World War and
how quickly it could be forgotten in the preparations for the
Second. Owen believed, as did most at the time, that he was
fighting in a 'war to end all wars', not because integrity and right

would replace evil, but because full realization of the horrors of this war would dissuade politicians from engaging in a subsequent one. He was, of course, quite wrong, and our ability to judge the poem in retrospect adds an irony to the optimistic spirit of the last three lines that Owen could not have guessed at.

The entire octave of the poem is comprised of a series of situations in which the soldiers appear to have come near to death. In order to make these scenes vivid or ironic—even humorous—Owen personifies Death. The fatalism of the poem is strengthened by the irony but through this Owen is still able to exercise his pity upon the soldiers who are forced to make a joke out of what they know to be a terrifying reality—as the epigraph from Sassoon illustrates.

The first line has an air of timorous bragging about it.

> Out there, we've walked quite friendly up to Death;

It is the tone that someone might employ when, safely out of danger, he recounts some act of bravado. The word 'friendly' is qualified by the preceding 'quite' which modifies the implied courage. But 'friendly' strengthens the effect of the personification by making Death seem more like a human to whom friendship can be offered. The same effect is continued in the second line where the apparent consciousness of sharing all their actions with ever-present Death—even the action of eating—gives the situation a vividly frightening tone. The idea develops into black humour even in the next line, where the sudden death of a comrade which has caused him to drop his mess-tin in the middle of eating is treated as a forgivable breach of decorum only. Again in line 4, the 'green thick odour of his breath' is forgiven because, after all, he *is* a friend of the soldiers. Even the spitting of bullets or the coughing of shrapnel or the skimming of his scythe are all over-looked because they come from an 'old friend'. Owen uses this irony to stress two points. One is the fact that since death is such a constant presence for the soldiers, they can adjust their lives to accept it and can react stoically to the 'closest-shaves' of death. Secondly, he is stressing the fatality of the men under these conditions. As death is an ever constant factor it is not, apparently, feared but accepted as an 'old chum', not through choice but because it is the soldiers' lot to live under such circumstances.

This same blasé attitude continues in the sestet, with the off-hand first line:

> Oh, Death was never enemy of ours!

They treat death with familiar indifference:

> We laughed at him, we leagued with him, old chum.

The notion of death being 'just a part of the job' is settled in the next line:

> No soldier's paid to kick against his powers.

Having used eleven lines of the sonnet to establish this tone of resolution to fate and death, Owen then demolishes the notion in three. In the last analysis, as these men know, Death is the *only* enemy. They laugh, but it is a frightened, if optimistic, laugh, for they 'know' that a time will come when the real 'war to end all wars' will be fought:

> We laughed, knowing that better men would come,
> And greater wars; . . .

The greater wars, they think, will be wars on Death itself, not on other men. The sense of the three lines may become clearer if 'in which' is momentarily substituted for 'when' in line 13:

> And greater wars; [in which] each proud fighter brags
> He wars on Death—for lives; not men—for flags.

The emptiness of the war's pursuits is made vividly clear from the last phrase—fighting 'men – for flags'. The soldiers look forward to a war in which the fighters might well be justifiably 'proud' and may rightfully brag that 'he wars on Death – for lives'.

Owen's optimism in this poem cannot be condemned. We may feel it a pity that he was deluded like the soldiers he writes about, but this does not alter the fact that the rightness of the pursuit of happy life and not death is to be aimed at. No matter what the conditions, even horrific acceptance of inevitable death, perhaps, as in the case of these men, where there is life there is hope.

A Brief Survey of Critical Opinion
Since 1920

There has been comparatively little written on Owen to date. Most of what has appeared has been praise, and little serious critical material exists. The best source of further reading at present, and until a complete bibliography of Owen's work becomes available, is *The New Cambridge Bibliography of English Literature* (*N.C.B.L.*), which lists the main works on Owen, or works containing significant sections about him, and also many relevant journal articles. There is to date no full scale biography of Owen as such, though Harold Owen's *Journey from Obscurity*[1] does give many details of his brother's life. For biographical details the *Dictionary of National Biography* which, like the *N.C.B.L.*, should be available in most large public libraries, is the best resort.

The year 1920 is chosen here as the date from which this brief review begins because in that year Owen's poems first emerged in book form, edited by Edith Sitwell and Siegfried Sassoon. This is not to say that none of Owen's poems had previously appeared. During his lifetime one had appeared in *The Hydra*, a magazine edited by Owen and published at Craiglockhart, and two in *The Nation*. Between his death and the publication of his poems in the 1920 edition, thirteen appeared in literary journals and magazines. It was the appearance of the collection of poems in 1920 that brought the first observations. *The Daily Chronicle* wrote on 8 December 1920.

> . . . we are bold enough to think and to say that the 'Poems' of Wilfred Owen . . . will emerge finally as the greatest of all poetry that derived its inspiration directly from the war. . . .

1 op. cit.

Though the *Times Literary Supplement* was baffled by some of Owen's challenging ideas, the most important defence of Owen came from J. Middleton Murry in his essay 'The Poet of the War', published in *Nation and Athenaeum*, where Owen was heralded as the finest poet of the war.

With the appearance of Edmund Blunden's edition of Owen in 1931, a fresh wave of critical interest broke. Distanced from the war by some twelve years, reactions tended to be more enthusiastic and less bewildered. Writing in the *New Statesman and Nation* of 11 April 1931, Richard Church stated:

> It is no easy matter to show in what way one discovers Owen to be more than merely a 'War Poet'. The gift of pure poetic genius is something we can talk about but cannot describe . . .

While this may seem too wildly adulatory, F. W. Bateson's comment that 'Wilfred Owen is the one modern poet whom it is impossible not to hear' (written in *English Poetry and the English Language, Oxford 1934*) is simply factually direct.

The poets of the 1930s, and Auden, Spender and Isherwood in particular, all admired Owen's poetry tremendously. In it they saw the struggle of one man against a militarist environment, and in the atmosphere of the 1930s with the rise of fascism throughout Europe, they identified with Owen in his struggle for peace and freedom. They looked on the Spanish Civil War in something of the light Owen imagined when he wrote at the end of 'The Next War':

> We laughed, knowing that better men would come,
> And greater wars; when each proud fighter brags
> He wars on Death—for lives; not men—for flags.

Owen's factual reporting of the war's horrors, his realistic language and his down-to-earth, unromantic imagery also appealed to them. Spender wrote of Owen in 1936[1]: '. . . One sees that Owen was already a poet of far deeper human understanding . . .' And in the same year, in his *New Literary Values*, David Daiches claimed:

[1] *The Destructive Element*, Steven Spender, Boston 1936.

... Eighteen years after Owen's ... death ... his reputation is greater than ever, and the power and cogency of what he has written remains as it will always remain ...

In 1934, C. Day Lewis's book *A Hope for Poetry* appeared and in it he placed Owen as one of the major influences upon what was then modern poetry, along with T. S. Eliot and Gerard Manley Hopkins.

The main voice of dissent in all this flow of praise came from W. B. Yeats when, in 1936 in his choice of poems to be included in the *Oxford Book of Modern Verse*, he excluded Owen. Yeats believed that Owen's type of poetry was morbid and ineffectual. On being asked for a war poem himself, he had written:

> I think it better that in times like these
> A poet's mouth be silent, for in truth
> We have no gift to set a statesman right.

He believed that Owen, in common with most war poets, had tried to look too deeply into the war, from which no useful results could emerge.

During the 1940s interest in Owen declined a little. Patricia Ledward, writing on 'The Poetry of Wilfred Owen' in *Poetry Review 32* for 1941, mentions that:

> In spite of his vivid and individual genius Owen seems to have been shamefully neglected. He is little spoken of, does not appear on many bookshelves, is seldom discussed as a possible influence on modern poetry.

Though she goes on to say '... with the possible exception of Siegfried Sassoon ... Owen stands out as the greatest war poet', in the rest of her essay she presents a very unexciting Owen indeed.

In 1945 Sassoon published his autobiography, *Siegfried's Journey*, in which he recalls his friendship with Owen from their meeting at Craiglockhart till their last parting. This book is invaluable as a background to Owen's most creative period and it presents a useful supplement to his letters of the period.

In 1946 in *Poetry Review 37* there appeared yet another article on Owen. Though only five years after the article by Miss Ledward in the same journal, this review follows a similar pattern of biography mixed in with vague passages of admiration, though Athalie Bushwell, the author, makes some interesting points.

The 1950s saw a slight revival of interest in Owen, with articles appearing more frequently. It is strange that, even as late as 1954, Howard Sergeant could be writing in *English* an article entitled 'The Importance of Wilfred Owen', which is almost purely biographical and which follows an identical pattern to both the *Poetry Review* contributions quoted above. Osbert Sitwell's *Noble Essences* appeared in 1950 but does not add much to the body of Owen criticism, dealing mainly with the man and touching on his poetry only in a non-specific way. In 1954, however, J. Cohen in an article entitled 'Owen's Greater Love' which appeared in *Tulane Studies in English*, mentions the dearth of actual analytical criticism on Owen, but for the main part his own contribution is too concerned with relating facts about Owen's Christian upbringing to his poetic imagery to supply us with some genuine analysis. V. de S. Pinto's *Crisis in English Poetry*, published in 1951, also contains references to Owen but none of the closely analytical kind.

It is not at all surprising that in the 1960s, with so much anti-war feeling in the air, with the threat of a new world war over Cuba in 1963 and the prolonged war in Vietnam, and with the disarmament campaigns that resulted from these threats, a renewed interest in Owen should occur. Many of the books with passages about him are vague and general in nature—though none the less interesting, as is *A Tribute to Owen* edited by T. J. Walsh, which appeared in 1964. But it was in 1960 that the only 'critical study' of Owen to emerge so far appeared. This was D. S. R. Welland's book, already mentioned. Though Dr. Welland may be said to be just slightly predisposed towards Owen, this does not blind his critical powers at all. This book deals thoroughly with most aspects of Owen's work. Perhaps the greatest advance is that Owen is examined as a poet and stands or falls on this alone. It certainly is the standard critical work at present.

In 1963 C. Day Lewis brought out a textually revised edition of the *Collected Poems*. Owen's study at both university and school level shows that his work is neither too simplistic nor too esoteric in its appeal. In 1975 he is a prescribed author for study at GCE level by four of the major Examination Boards and is on the syllabus of most general poetry courses at British universities. There is no better proof of the continued interest displayed in this poet whose 'greater love' and unselfconscious compassion is one of the strongest appeals for peace we have.

Bibliography

Editions
Poems (ed.) Edmund Blunden, Chatto and Windus. First published in 1931—reprinted regularly to date.
Collected Poems (ed.) C. Day Lewis, Chatto and Windus. First published in 1963—reprinted regularly to date.

Bibliography
New Cambridge Bibliography of English Literature, Cambridge University Press, 1964.
White, William, *Wilfred Owen (1893–1918): A Bibliography*, Kent State University Press, U.S.A., 1965.

Letters
Wilfred Owen: The Collected Letters (ed.) Harold Owen and John Bell, Oxford University Press, 1967.

Biographical Material
Hibberd, Dominic, *Wilfred Owen, War Poems and Others*, Chatto and Windus, 1973. (Also contains Owen's poems based largely on the C. Day Lewis edition, and has some notes on the poems. A useful book to read in connection with Owen.)
Owen, Harold, *Journey from Obscurity: Wilfred Owen 1893–1918, Memoirs of the Owen Family*, Oxford University Press, 1963–65.
Owen, Harold, *Aftermath*, Oxford University Press, 1970.
Sassoon, Siegfried, *Siegfried's Journey 1916–20*, 1945.
Sitwell, Osbert, *Noble Essences*, 1950.
Walsh, T. J. (ed.) *A Tribute to Wilfred Owen*, 1964.

Critical Material
Bergonzi, Bernard, *Heroes' Twilight: A Study of the Literature of the Great War*, 1965.
Davidson, Mildred, *The Poetry is the Pity*, Chatto and Windus, 1961.

Grubb, Frederick, *A Vision of Reality: A study in Liberalism in Twentieth-century Verse*, 1965.

Johnson, John H., *English Poetry of the First World War: A Study in the Evolution of Lyric and Narrative Form, 1964.*

Silkin, Jon, *Out of Battle: The Poetry of the Great War*, 1972.

Thwaite, Anthony, *Contemporary English Poetry: An Introduction*, 1959.

Welland, D. S. R., *Wilfred Owen: A Critical Study*, 1960.

White, G. M., *Wilfred Owen*, U.S.A., 1969.

Anthologies Containing some of Owen's Poetry

Gardner, Brian (ed.) *Up the Line to Death: The War Poets, 1914–18*, 1964.

Parsons, I. M. (ed.) *Men Who March Away: Poems of the First World War*, 1965.

The Oxford Book of Twentieth Century Verse, Oxford University Press, 1973.

Penguin Books of English Verse, Penguin, 1964.

(*Note:* There are many anthologies which contain poems by Owen, and this list only gives cases where more than only one or two of the very best known poems are printed.)

Index of Poems and First Lines